color lines and
racial angles

the society pages

The Social Side of Politics

Crime and the Punished

Color Lines and Racial Angles

the
society
pages

color lines and racial angles

douglas hartmann
UNIVERSITY OF MINNESOTA

christopher uggen
UNIVERSITY OF MINNESOTA

w. w. norton & company

NEW YORK | LONDON

W. W. Norton & Company has been independent since its founding in 1923, when William Warder Norton and Mary D. Herter Norton first published lectures delivered at the People's Institute, the adult education division of New York City's Cooper Union. The firm soon expanded its program beyond the Institute, publishing books by celebrated academics from America and abroad. By mid-century, the two major pillars of Norton's publishing program—trade books and college texts—were firmly established. In the 1950s, the Norton family transferred control of the company to its employees, and today—with a staff of four hundred and a comparable number of trade, college, and professional titles published each year—W. W. Norton & Company stands as the largest and oldest publishing house owned wholly by its employees.

Book Design: Isaac Tobin
Composition: Westchester Book Composition
Manufacturing: Courier-Westford
Production Manager: Sean Mintus

ISBN: 978-0-393-92039-0

Library of Congress Cataloging-in-Publication Data

Color lines and racial angles / [edited by] Douglas Hartmann, University of Minnesota, Christopher Uggen, University of Minnesota.—First edition.
      pages cm.—(The society pages)
   Includes bibliographical references and index.
   ISBN 978-0-393-92039-0 (pbk. : alk. paper)
  1. United States—Ethnic relations—History—21st century.   2. United States—Race relations—History—21st century.   3. Cultural pluralism—United States—History—21st century.   4. Minorities—United States—Social conditions—21st century.   5. Racism—Social aspects—United States—History—21st century.   6. Group identity—United States—History—21st century.   I. Hartmann, Douglas.   II. Uggen, Christopher.
   E184.A1C544   2014
   305.800973—dc23

                                                                    2014018417

W. W. Norton & Company, Inc., 500 Fifth Avenue, New York, NY 10110-0017
www.wwnorton.com
W. W. Norton & Company, Ltd., Castle House, 75/76 Wells Street, London
W1T3QT

thesocietypages.org

contents

Series Preface

DOUGLAS HARTMANN AND CHRISTOPHER UGGEN   xi

Introduction

DOUGLAS HARTMANN AND CHRISTOPHER UGGEN   xv

Changing Lenses: Diversity at the Derby

DOUGLAS HARTMANN WITH WING YOUNG HUIE   xxv

part 1 core contributions   1

1   **The Uncertain Future of Race in America**

KIA HEISE AND DOUGLAS HARTMANN   3

2   **Social Fact: The Homicide Divide**

LAUREN J. KRIVO AND JULIE A. PHILLIPS   21

3   **Asian American Exceptionalism and "Stereotype Promise"**

JENNIFER LEE   27

4   **Latinos, Biculturalism, and the In-Between**
WENDY ROTH   49

5   **Beyond the Big, Bad Racist**
MATTHEW W. HUGHEY   65

part 2   cultural contexts   81

6   **White Trash: The Social Origins of a Stigmatype**
MATT WRAY   83

7   **The Fascination and Frustration with Native American Mascots**
JENNIFER GUILIANO   95

8   **Environmental Inequalities**
HOLLIE NYSETH BREHM AND DAVID N. PELLOW   115

9   **Thinking about Trayvon with Charles A. Gallagher, Zenzele Isoke, Enid Logan, and Aldon Morris**
STEPHEN SUH   133

part 3 critical takes 153

10 American Immigration and Forgetting, with Yen Le Espiritu, Katherine Fennelly, and Douglas S. Massey
STEPHEN SUH 155

11 Color Blindness vs. Race Consciousness— An American Ambivalence
MEGHAN A. BURKE 165

12 Exposing *The New Jim Crow* with Michelle Alexander
KIA HEISE 177

13 Diversity and the New CEOs
RICHARD L. ZWEIGENHAFT AND G. WILLIAM DOMHOFF 191

Discussion Guide and Group Activities 207
About the Contributors 213
Index 217

series preface

DOUGLAS HARTMANN AND CHRISTOPHER UGGEN

It started with a conversation about record labels. Our favorite imprints are known for impeccable taste, creative design, and an eye for both quality and originality. They consistently deliver the best work by the most original voices. Wouldn't it be cool if W. W. Norton & Company and TheSocietyPages.org joined forces to develop a book series with the same goals in mind?

The Society Pages is a multidisciplinary online hub bringing fresh social scientific knowledge and insight to the broadest public audiences in the most open, accessible, and timely manner possible. The largest, most visible collection of sociological material on the web (currently drawing about a million hits every month), TSP is composed of a family of prolific blogs and bloggers, podcasts, interviews, exchanges, teaching content, reading recommendations, and original peer-reviewed features. The TSP book series, published in collaboration with W. W. Norton, assembles the best original content from the website in key thematic collections. With contributions from leading scholars, snippets from the site's influential "Community Pages," and a provocative collection of discussion topics and group activities, this innovative new series provides an accessible and affordable entry point for strong sociological perspectives on topics of immediate social import and public relevance.

The third volume in this series tackles race, ethnicity, and diversity in contemporary American society. As with our previous volumes, the chapters are organized into three main sections. "Core Contributions" exemplify how sociologists and other social scientists think about race-related groups and topics—in this case the demographics of race, the construction of group identities, and the social psychology of prejudice and racism. Chapters in the "Cultural Contexts" section engage race and diversity in and through cultural realms—ranging from mass media and sports to the environment—in which powerful racial dimensions are sometimes overlooked. Finally, the "Critical Takes" chapters provide sociological commentary, perspective, and reflections on the problematic structure and future of race relations in the United States.

Each of these concise, accessible chapters reflects TSP's distinctive tone and style. As with other books in the series, this volume features contributions from the TSP Social Facts crew headed by Debby Carr and the Changing Lenses Project. Sprinkled throughout are "TSP Tie-Ins," connecting the chapters to content on our website, including Community Pages like Cyborgology, Girl w/ Pen, and Lisa Wade and Gwen Sharp's wildly popular and well-respected Sociological Images. The volume concludes with a Discussion Guide and Group Activities that challenge readers to draw connections among the chapters, think more deeply and critically about race in social life, and link to ongoing conversations and interactive posts online.

introduction

DOUGLAS HARTMANN AND CHRISTOPHER UGGEN

The power of racial identities and the persistence of deep racial inequalities are among the greatest puzzles and frustrations of a nation that believes itself to be color-blind, celebrates individualism, and otherwise flaunts itself as a bastion of equality and opportunity. And race is core sociological terrain. Sociologists have long been leaders in researching and teaching on race, racial inequalities, and racism itself—the go-to, trusted source for social facts, analysis, and commentary on all topics race-related in the United States. Also, given that we've had tons of great racial content and commentary on the site and that both of us have done a fair bit of research and writing in the area ourselves, there was never any doubt that we'd end up creating a TSP/Norton volume on race. It was a no-brainer. The only questions were when we would do it and how it would be organized.

What made these choices particularly challenging is that there is so much ground to cover when it comes to race in the United States. In a very basic but fundamental way, race seems to be everywhere, yet many Americans have a very difficult time acknowledging race, recognizing its impacts, or even talking about it. History is also a key dimension—the history of slavery and Jim Crow segregation as well as the civil rights movement, various waves of immigration policy and reform, and the rise of multiculturalism. When we talk about race, we refer not only to a number of different groups with a range of experiences, histories, and problems, but also to a whole system of social relationships and ways of looking at society. To capture and dissect all of the empirical dimensions of race, sociologists have deployed a range of classic terms and conceptions—including prejudice, discrimination, assimilation, and race relations—as well as emerging ideas and research paradigms including whiteness and white privilege, color blindness, and the whole discourse of diversity. And this isn't even to mention the broader implications and consequences of race in the culture at large. To put all of this in a slim volume of a dozen or so short chapters became the *real* challenge.

Thus, we took a different approach to putting this volume together. Rather than attempt to assemble the volume out of the (too many) pieces we had in hand, we sat down with our graduate students (several of whom were beginning to teach their own classes in the area) and imagined the volume we wanted to use in our classrooms. Here's what we envisioned:

- We wanted a volume that highlighted the most provocative, productive new thinking on race—emerging work on whiteness and white privilege, color blindness, and diversity, as well as powerful cultural critiques of racial stereotypes that circulate in contemporary culture and mass media.

- We wanted a volume that would include and illustrate core sociological contributions to the study of race, ethnicity, and diversity; the social construction of race; the importance of group formation and collective identity, as well as of the relationships among groups; and the power of prejudice, discrimination, and privilege.

- We wanted to see chapters on a range of racial-minority groups and their unique experiences but also a broad conceptual overview of the construction, experience, and consequence of race in contemporary America.

- We wanted a book with both conceptual and empirical chapters, written by both established, big-name scholars, as well as exciting up-and-coming researchers.

- We wanted a book that captured the dynamics of racial phenomena alongside the broader, pervasive, and consequential impacts of race in contemporary society, even in areas and arenas not usually thought of as impacted by race.

- And above all else, we wanted a book that captured and conveyed how sociologists think about and study race and its repercussions in the U.S. today.

With this big vision in mind, we went back to TheSocietyPages.org to seek out the articles and posts that best exemplified what we wanted to see in our "ideal race reader." Where we found holes, we recruited leading scholars to fill out our volume. The result, we think, is a clear and incisive book that covers all the bases. We find it provocative, accessible, and useful, and we hope our readers will, too.

section-by-section organization

Color Lines and Racial Angles is organized in three main sections, each of which highlights distinctive aspects of the sociological vision of and approach to the study of race and diversity in contemporary American society.

CORE CONTRIBUTIONS

Sociology is an empirical pursuit—an engagement with society as it is—and some of the most basic contributions that sociologists have to make to the study of race involve facts about demographics, the actual experiences of specific communities of color, and the social forces that shape and determine each. The chapters collected in this section represent these core contributions.

Hartmann and Kia Heise begin with an overview of how the changing demographics of the American populace are remaking American racial categories and relationships, and Lauren Krivo and Julie Phillips document the outrageous disparities in U.S. homicide victimization. These chapters go beyond describing racial differences: Chapter 1, for instance, explores some of the social and cultural factors that will influence how changing demographics unfold in lived experiences. Chapter 3, by Jennifer Lee, doesn't just say that Asian American images and stereotypes are unique; rather, it reveals how model minority stereotypes pressure young Asian Americans with what she calls "stereotype promise." And in Chapter 4, Wendy Roth discusses the different ways in which Latinos understand biculturalism and their in-between social status in the U.S., unpacking the racial category we so often and so uncritically think of as "Hispanic."

Finally, Matt Hughey's provocative "Beyond the Big, Bad Racist" shifts the lens to look at one of sociology's other primary foci for the study of race: the attitudes, stereotypes, and actions that mark racial differences and the inequalities that go along with them. The most conventional analytic terms here are *prejudice* and *discrimination,* but to this conceptual toolkit Hughey adds a focus on white identity and privilege. Hughey challenges us to think about the persistence of racial categories and inequalities from the viewpoint of the privileged—those who receive preferential outcomes even when they aren't intended or desired. He ends up with a challenging new definition and conception of racism.

CULTURAL CONTEXTS

Race, at least in the United States, is one of those social phenomena whose impacts extend well beyond its explicit boundaries and borders. Its dynamics are reflected and reproduced in—and, in turn, affect—all aspects of social life, from the most mundane, everyday interactions to the biggest political theater, from personal experiences to public events and all manner of historical change. The chapters in this section highlight the contours of phemonena that might not otherwise be seen as racial.

The first in this set, from Matt Wray, takes us on a quick sociological tour of the origins and impact of the term "white trash." With characteristic panache, Wray shows how the emergence and evolution of this term has been shaped by the dynamics of class, gender, and sexuality (as well as race)—

and, in the process, suggests some disturbing consequences and outcomes of the term for policies relating to health and reproduction of poor whites and other racialized groups. With a similarly broad historical and cultural orientation, Jennifer Guiliano introduces us to the world of racist sports mascots in Chapter 7. She highlights the history, complexity, and tragedy of the Native American experience in American culture, while reminding us of the importance of popular cultural practices for reproducing and contesting racial stereotypes and images.

Chapter 8's authors, Hollie Nyseth Brehm and David N. Pellow, are experts in environmental sociology and global social movements. Their contribution highlights just a few of the many ways race structures our experience and understanding of space, place, and the distribution of environmental resources in contemporary society. This piece is a compelling example of how sociologists train a racial lens onto social domains that might not otherwise or automatically be seen to have racial dimensions or implications.

The final chapter in this section is a roundtable exchange among a power-packed group of commentators reflecting on Trayvon Martin's death and the media coverage and public commentary that followed. This chapter illustrates timeless sociological points and provides an excellent and provocative example of sociologists' critical orientation.

CRITICAL TAKES

Because they document the facts, dynamics, and broader impacts of social life, sociologists are well positioned to offer critical commentary and analysis on the world as it is. Indeed, much of the content on The Society Pages is devoted to this kind of interpretative and critically reflective work.

In the first piece in this section, Stephen Suh brings together an all-star cast of experts—Yen Espiritu, Kathy Fennelly, and Doug Massey—to talk about immigration and its sometimes forgotten or underestimated importance for race relations in U.S. history. In the context of today's politically charged debates about immigration, this exchange reminds us of our country's melting-pot past and the troubling implications of having forgotten our history.

Chapter 11 grows out of Meghan Burke's new work on racial discourse, taking critical, sociological analysis and thinking in several new directions. Through her research in racially diverse communities, Burke calls attention to the contradictions between the color-blind ideologies and discourses held by so many Americans and how these are also blind to the persistent realities of race. Burke complicates the picture by documenting the newly trumpeted values of diversity and multiculturalism, showing how Americans are gripped by a profound "ambivalence" about their own racial realities and ideals. She challenges us to reconcile our aspirations with the realities of race in a diverse society.

Next, Kia Heise's interview with law professor and civil rights lawyer Michelle Alexander, the author of the best-selling *The New Jim Crow*, also makes a critical intervention in the area of criminal justice policy. Excerpted from a longer "Office Hours" podcast on the TSP website, this exchange introduces Alexander's argument that criminal punishment has succeeded slavery and legal discrimination as a system of racial control and touches on the grassroots social movement for carceral change.

The volume concludes with Richard Zweigenhaft and Bill Domhoff detailing the experience of the unique—and uniquely successful—individuals who have made it into the higher echelons of power and privilege. Drawing from their years of research on the select group of American CEOs who do *not* hail from privileged, white backgrounds, the authors highlight the United States' progress in race relations since the civil rights movement while illuminating the barriers that stand in the way of progress for so many.

Whether in the classroom or the public square, calls for a "conversation about race" are meaningless without basic knowledge and understanding. This volume specifically identifies big, difficult discussions, while giving voice to a diversity of perspectives and positions on them. We like to think it might spur some better-informed and more productive conversations about race in contemporary American society.

As always, we must express our gratitude to the University of Minnesota, W. W. Norton & Company (in particular, the sociology editor, Karl Bakeman), and The Society Pages' graduate student board, several of whom are included as authors in this volume. Hollie Nyseth Brehm is our project's graduate editor. Kia Heise and Lisa Gulya were the graduate editors of this volume (with some early assistance from Stephen Suh), and they authored the Discussion Guide and TSP Tie-Ins found throughout. Our associate editor and producer is the incomparable Letta Page.

changing lenses: diversity at the derby

DOUGLAS HARTMANN WITH WING YOUNG HUIE

Wing Young Huie: I had never been to rural Montana. When we first pulled into Baker, it resembled a scene from an apocalyptic movie: tidy, rustic shops lined Main Street, but where was everybody? A lone soul finally appeared to inform us that the demolition derby was in town. Apparently the entire populace of Baker was at this car-as-gladiator spectacle.

An accommodating elderly gentleman in a cowboy hat excitedly explained the intricacies of the sport to us. The sight and sounds of smashing metal contrasted with the languorous audience and its intermittent cheers. In many ways, it didn't seem all that different from a crowd at a baseball game back in the Twin Cities.

When my attention turned to photographic possibilities, I was excited to spy one of the only Asian faces in this communal gathering. This man and his wife, both Cambodian, blended right in with their dress and deportment. But to me, he still looks Photoshopped into this picture. I wonder: is that what I, also an Asian American, look like walking around the land of Lake

changing lenses: diversity at the derby

Wobegon—as though I've been Photoshopped into the landscape?

Doug Hartmann: This was one of the first photos Wing and I workshopped publicly as we began the Changing Lenses project. On that winter night, I told the crowd that I liked the *idea* of this photograph as much as the image itself. It so powerfully and succinctly captured the reality of an increasingly diverse, multicultural America. As I put it then: "What could be more mainstream, Midwest, Heartland-America than a demolition derby?" And yet, here in the midst of this quintessentially middle-American spectacle, was an Asian American man.

I think I went on to talk about the paradoxes, complexities, and peculiarities of America and race—giving examples from my own projects, Wing's portfolio, and other scholarly research. I think I talked about the tensions between our easy celebration of diversity and the problems and inequalities that persist even in the face of these differences—what my colleague Joyce Bell and I have called America's "happy talk" about diversity. I think I even brought up the question of whether Americans' encounters with racial others serve to break down traditional racial and ethnic boundaries or simply reinforce them.

But honestly, what I most remember about the event was not what Wing and I said about this photo; it was the audience response. They had vast and radically contrasting things to say. People talked about class differences and rural/urban contrasts, pointed out the different levels of interest and attention among the spectators, and expressed extremely different views on the Asian man himself. Some saw him as alienated and out of place, others thought he looked so confident and self-assured he might be in charge of the whole operation. One audience member looked into the background and took the conversation into the controversies surrounding public breastfeeding, while another spotted a woman in the crowd and simply pointed out that she looked like his grandmother, so he felt kind toward her.

This conversation reminded me that diversity isn't just a socio-demographic phenomenon, but that there is a diversity of opinion in the various ways people see and experience the worlds in which we live. This is a general point, of course, but a crucial one for this project. Rich images like those Wing Young Huie produces remind us of the complexity of social life—an idea that is powerfully conveyed when you invite folks to respond to and comment upon your work, as both artists and academics do every day.

core contributions

the uncertain future of race in america

KIA HEISE AND DOUGLAS HARTMANN

You've probably heard by now: according to official Census projections and other sources, the United States will be a "majority-minority" society by 2050 (if not sooner). That is, the traditional "Anglo-Saxon/white" majority will be outnumbered by those who are not white. This transition is well under way, and in many places it is already a *fait accompli*. Nearly a quarter of states have already "achieved" majority-minority status or will soon get there, and within 35 years or so, the proportion of U.S. Latino/as will nearly double (from 16 to 30% of the population), and 8% of Americans will be of Asian origin (up from about 5% currently).

Basic demographic trends account for the bulk of these transformations: large numbers of immigrants have come into the country in the last few decades, non-Hispanic white women are experiencing declining birth rates, and there is a new baby boom among new immigrant groups and other communities of color. But demographics are not destiny. Sociologists know that a host of sociological variables—ranging from how various communities of color identify themselves and how they and their children will engage mainstream society to the reactions of the existing white majority and the country's economy—will shape and determine how these changes unfold and their impacts on racial classification and race relations in the United States. Depending upon their analysis of these myriad forces and trends, sociologists who study race and demographics envision a wide range of scenarios for America's racial future.

blurring or hardening

Richard Alba is both a leading voice and among the most optimistic of those sociologists who research race in the United States. Alba believes the country is entering a new era of opportunity, mobility, and growth for new immigrants and historic racial minority communities that will result in the "blurring" of traditional racial categories and boundaries in the country. In Alba's scenario, changing demographics are most likely to break down traditional color lines and racial barriers and open up the possibility of a more integrated society.

Alba's vision of a less racialized America stems from two main sources. One is his analysis (with Victor Nee in their award-winning book *Remaking the American Mainstream*) of the characteristics and behaviors of new immigrant groups—their tremendous socioeconomic mobility, for instance, as well as intermarriage, residential integration, and how quickly immigrants learn English and accommodate themselves to American culture. Simply because of their continuing accomplishment and assimilation, new immigrants are calling into question and fundamentally changing prevailing racial hierarchies and stereotypes (and diversifying mainstream culture in the process).

The second reason for Alba's optimism is his understanding and further analysis of the opportunities presented by current economic projections and demographics. For Alba, an expanding global economy, the exit of baby boomers from the labor force, and the declining birth rates of the majority-white group together create conditions in which "members of lower-situated groups can move upward without affecting the life chances of members of more established ones." This is what Alba calls "non-zero-sum mobility"—mobility that doesn't provoke the competitive backlash that new immigrants often encounter—and it essentially describes the situation for ethnic European immigrants a little over one hundred years ago. Although Irish, Italian, and other Southern and Eastern European immigrants were originally seen as racially different, they encountered a booming post-war economy and benefited from restrictive policies that sharply curtailed immigration after their arrival. Over time, these once "different" immigrants were able to assimilate—or "become white"—and thus overcome the boundaries and barriers of color. Alba is more cautious about the color lines that confront individuals from other, historically disadvantaged minority groups (especially African Americans); however, he remains hopeful that with proper education and social support America is looking at a future of softening and blurring of racial boundaries.

Other sociologists are far less optimistic. They envision either the reinforcement—or "hardening"—of existing racial barriers, or the emergence of new racial lines and cultural categories. Eduardo Bonilla-Silva is a sociologist who sees both of these trends on the horizon. For Bonilla-Silva race is a system of relationships between advantaged and disadvantaged groups in which those who are advantaged by existing racial systems are more likely to close ranks against racial outsiders than they are to relinquish the privileges that go along with their race. Bonilla-Silva believes the most prominent and problematic racial boundaries and barriers—especially those associated with privilege and power—will calcify rather than soften. Whites, essentially, will cling to privilege and the racial status quo will be reproduced.

Because of their basic assumptions about competition and social closure, many sociological analysts agree. But what makes Bonilla-Silva's approach unique is his belief that the reproduction of racial categories and inequalities now and in the future is and will be driven less by old-fashioned prejudice than, ironically, by the color-blind ideals to which Americans of all racial backgrounds adhere.

Many Americans, according to Bonilla-Silva (as well as to Meghan Burke elsewhere in this volume), claim not to "see race." They say they make decisions on whom to befriend, date, and hire based on character alone. While the notion that Americans *should* be color-blind—that race should not matter—has a long and potentially progressive legacy, scholars like Bonilla-Silva and Burke insist "color-blind" is far from an accurate depiction of the United States. In this context, the fact that so many Americans refuse to "see" race makes it very difficult to face the inequalities that continue to accompany skin color. In other words, the conviction that the United States is already color-blind makes it nearly impossible for Americans to acknowledge and address the inequalities that go along with racial differences in this society.

It's not that Bonilla-Silva sees no change on the horizon. Alongside the entrenchment of current majority-minority lines, Bonilla-Silva also predicts the emergence of new racial categories and identifiers that go beyond the traditional black-white dualisms. In particular, as Bonilla-Silva sees it, the explosion of Latino immigration, the evolving status of immigrant groups like Asian Americans, and increases in interracial dating and mixed-race children is completely remaking and reshaping American racial categories. In this way, the United States is evolving from a biracial system of "white" and "nonwhite" to a tri-racial system of "white," "honorary white," and "collective black."

Bonilla-Silva's three-category schema resembles the hierarchy in many Latin American countries. And just as many Latin American cultures tend to downplay the colonial legacies of privilege for those with lighter skin tones, Bonilla-Silva suggests that color blindness will do the same in the U.S. Even those at the bottom of this racial stratification system will refuse to identify in racialized terms, preferring instead to claim national unity—"We are all Puerto Rican," for example. But such ideals and identifications obscure the deeper realities of race. A new racial landscape will appear more fluid and multicultural, but Bonilla-Silva argues that it will actually be *more* tilted toward white privilege in that it will discourage talking about race at all. It will quietly encourage racial minorities in their struggle to become "white."

class and the lines of color and culture

It is often assumed that the U.S. is a land of opportunity and upward mobility. However, downward mobility is also always a possibility, and sociological research suggests that this trajectory is more likely for certain racial groups and immigrant communities than others. The notion of downward mobility, introduced into the study of race by a sociologist named Herbert Gans, suggests another way to think about changing color lines.

Essentially, Gans insisted that racial categories are defined not only by skin color but also by class and especially by culture—that is, whether groups are perceived as "respectable." As whites become a numerical minority, according to Gans, they may seek out cultural allies in other groups constructed as "non-black," strengthening that binary boundary. Writing at the end of the 1970s, Gans predicted that the boundaries between middle-class and affluent Asian Americans and whites would continue to weaken. White America sees upwardly mobile Asian Americans as "model minorities" (they appear to share the dominant, white culture's values and norms). And yet, they remain in danger of losing their honorary white status if they pose a threat to the interests of white Americans. This type of racial hierarchy would look similar to many black Americans—they're likely to remain on the bottom. What would be different is that new immigrants with darker skin or different cultural backgrounds would join—or be joined to—the black Americans in the lowest social position.

Gans predicted that those not fitting into the black or non-black categories would inhabit a residual or middle category from which they could move into either category, depending on whether they were deemed "black" or "non-black" by the dominant population. This category might include lower-class members of racially acceptable groups and higher-class members of racially stigmatized groups. Upward social mobility on a large scale would allow a group to advance farther from the black group and closer to the non-black group. But a significant change in the class status of an entire racial minority group would require a healthy economy that allowed for upward mobility. Still, Gans pointed to the faulty assumption that the processes of assimilation and mobility are joined: economic prosperity does not guarantee the acceptance of any group.

This more multifaceted, class-inflected conception of American racial hierarchies has helped define a third version of America's racial future that Alejandro Portes and Min Zhou have called "segmented assimilation." Focusing on how second-generation immigrants fit into society, Portes and Zhou argue that young U.S. immigrants can either join (or be joined to) the upwardly mobile middle class or to the racialized and marginalized inner-city communities in which many new immigrants live. The direction they travel along these paths influences their future prospects (including educational attainment and career success). Children of immigrants must immediately get on a path toward a college education to prevent becoming "stuck" in the low-paying job market of the urban underclass.

Because of their geographic location and the racial stereotypes they encounter, downward assimilation is a significant concern in this vision. If immigrants of color are restricted in their educational and career prospects, the underclass will grow, further separating the largely white middle class from poor people of color, both economically and socially. This reality would not improve race relations. Taking segmented assimilation patterns into consideration, Portes and Ruben Rumbaut argue that traditional assimilation is not always the best path for immigrants, especially those who are poor or more likely to be discriminated against. New immigrants and their children are more likely to receive material and moral support within ethnic enclaves, where community support and the acquisition of "mainstream" skills can lead to upward mobility. So instead of just a racial hierarchy with one group on the top and one on the bottom, Portes and his collaborators envision a racial system defined by an established and upwardly mobile class, a permanent underclass category, and a range of more or less unique, culturally distinct ethnic communities fitting somewhere in between.

other underlying factors

Many sociologists are hesitant to predict which of the preceding pathways and patterns will hold sway for America's racial future. But no matter what future is envisioned, there are a number of underlying factors that will drive the shape of racial categories and relationships to come. Changes in immigration policy (such as those debated in Congress in the summer and fall of 2013) would obviously complicate things dramatically. Education and job training are even more fundamental. Communities of color tend to be among the least advantaged, most marginal groups in American society. In 2010, for example, 39% of African American children, 34% of Hispanic children, and 38% of Native American children lived in poverty (compared with 18% of white children and 13.5% of Asian American kids). Without proper—and probably *better*—education and job training, these young people will not be able to fill the positions made available by baby boomer retirement and the expansion of the economy. Such stagnation would reinforce, rather than challenge, existing racial categories and hierarchies.

Increases in interracial dating and mixed-race children also complicate any predictions for the future of racial categories in the United States. The percentage of people in interracial marriages more than doubled from 1980 to 2010. Currently, 8.4% of U.S. marriages are interracial. In states with larger populations of Hispanic and Asian immigrants, people are more likely to marry outside of their race, and they are most likely to marry whites: 43% of interracial marriages were white-Hispanic couples, 14% were white-Asian couples, and 12% were white-black couples.

According to the 2010 Census, there are 9 million mixed-race individuals in the United States. We don't know how these Americans or their children will identify in coming years—whether it's with an existing racial category or with newly emergent "mixed race" classifications (or even some other, emerging labels). Many demographic projections assume people of color will continue to identify in the same ways they have in previous decades. Yet this is not necessarily the case. The rise of Native American populations in the 1960s and '70s, as scholars such as Joane Nagel and Stephen Cornell have shown, resulted not from demographic changes but from identity changes: more Americans named and claimed a Native identity. Mary Waters has written about how new, first-generation African immigrants see American racial hierarchies and are resisting being lumped in with

African Americans (though members of the second and third generations exhibit much different patterns). And, as Wendy Roth details elsewhere in this volume, individuals of Hispanic origin exhibit several different self-labeling strategies—a dominant one being the emergence of a new Latino racial classification.

Among the myriad other factors impacting the future of race in the U.S., let us not overlook the reaction and response of those who have historically benefited most from racial differences and hierarchies.

white reaction and response

Some white Americans believe these demographic changes are cause for celebration, while others see the changes as threats that need to be contained. The most outspoken of the latter believe white American culture and the white population as we know it today are worth preserving, not only for nostalgia's sake, but also for the economic and political good of the nation.

White nativists think the U.S. was founded on cultural principles that will be tarnished by a too racially disparate nation. It is not uncommon to hear older white Americans pine for the long-lost "real" America. Underneath this desire is often the sense that white Americans have lost control—expressed commonly in protest signs calling for a movement to "Take Our Country Back." Even among whites who harbor no conscious racial anxiety, the coming demographic changes will require a shift in thought: they will no longer be "raceless" because of their normality. White will necessarily become an expressed racial category. While white racial anxiety is not new—whites have been afraid of losing their privileged status since the days of slavery—the strong, taken-for-granted link between "white" and "American" is weakening for the first time in U.S. history.

White anxieties are most visible among vocal conservative pundits. On election night 2012, Bill O'Reilly, a Fox News television host, reported that Barack Obama had only won the presidency because he pandered to female, black, and Latino voters (he seemed to think no rational white male would vote for Obama). "Traditional America," O'Reilly argued, was being destroyed: the "white establishment is now the minority." Glenn Beck, a former Fox News personality and talk-radio host, famously called Obama a racist in 2009, claiming he held "a deep-seated hatred for white people or white culture." And in 2010, commenting on the educational benefits promised to young immigrants in the DREAM Act, Beck claimed, if you are "a white American citizen, you're pretty much toast."

Other political pundits express fears that new immigrants will fail to assimilate properly and thus break down traditional American culture. Pat Buchanan, a conservative commentator and three-time presidential candidate, has written extensively about his anxieties over the end of white American culture. In a chapter from his book *Suicide of a Superpower: Will America Survive to 2025?* entitled "The End of White America," Buchanan claims white Americans are an "endangered species." By 2050 (that magical majority-minority date), Buchanan opines, "America will be more of a Third World than a Western nation, as 54% of the 435 million people in the United States . . . will trace their roots to Asia, Africa, and Latin America."

The sense of white anxiety is especially apparent in the intense opposition to affirmative action programs. In just one example, Proposition 209 (also known as the California Civil Rights Initiative) amended the California state constitution in November 1996 to prohibit affirmative action based on gender, race, or ethnicity in the areas of public employment, contracting, or education. Again, the majority of white voters (62%), especially white men, turned out in favor of the amendment. More recently, a suit brought by a white student against the University of Texas and hinging on its affirmative action program made it all the way to the U.S. Supreme Court. An African American president notwithstanding, whites remain "on top" by all indictors of success. But the increasing sense of white victimhood has led to ever-louder accusations of "reverse racism" in education, employment, and politics. The sense that America is a white nation is still very much with us.

It's worth noting that all these fears, while offensive to many, are not necessarily unfounded. A white majority *has* always dominated the U.S. power structure and set the tone for political and social norms, as seen in Richard L. Zweigenhaft and G. William Domhoff's chapter in this book. White supremacy was explicit in the law until the 1960s, and white politicians, leaders, advertisers, and CEOs have been able to create and disseminate white-centric ideals, regardless of the law. Those who fear the coming demographic changes are most likely overestimating how *much* power white people will lose—after all, most states will remain majority white for many generations to come—but they're not wrong in noting that the white worldview will lose at least some of its dominance. The mystery is what whiteness will mean if and when "white" is just another race in the U.S.

———

A whole range of possible racial futures lies ahead of us. The majority of Americans claim to want a society free of racism and appreciative of diversity, but they disagree, sometimes vehemently, over how to achieve that goal. The culture of color blindness identified by Eduardo Bonilla-Silva is a blessing and a curse. The ideology can be one of opportunity and equality for all, regardless of culture, skin color, or creed. But it can also be a binding rhetoric that blinds its adherents to the change, as well as to the persistent inequalities and barriers of race. Even in the most optimistic scenario (Alba's), significant attention must be paid to enhancing the educational opportunities for racially marginalized groups.

We must see and acknowledge changes in racial categories and race relations—not only to better understand our future but also to try to shape and mold our society according to our highest aspirations and ideals.

RECOMMENDED READING

Richard Alba. 2009. *Blurring the Color Line: The New Chance for a More Integrated America*, Cambridge, MA: Harvard University Press.

Eduardo Bonilla-Silva. 2009. *Racism without Racists: Color-blind Racism and the Persistence of Racial Inequality in the United States* (2nd edition), Boulder, CO: Rowman & Littlefield.

Herbert J. Gans. 1992. "Second-generation Decline: Scenarios for the Economic and Ethnic Futures of the Post-1965 American Immigrants," *Ethnic & Racial Studies* 15(2):173–192.

Jennifer Lee and Frank D. Bean. 2010. *The Diversity Paradox: Immigration and the Color Line in 21st Century America*, New York: Russell Sage Foundation.

Alejandro Portes and Min Zhou. 1993. "The New Second Generation: Segmented Assimilation and Its Variants among Post-1965 Immigrant Youth," *Annual American Academy of Political and Social Science* 530:74–96.

social fact:
the homicide divide

LAUREN J. KRIVO AND JULIE A. PHILLIPS

The United States has a long and troubled history with violence, from the slaughtering of the American Indians to the American Revolution to the gun culture of the Wild West (that, in many ways, still remains). Comparisons with other wealthy, English-speaking nations such as Australia, Ireland, and the United Kingdom highlight the country's unique position: levels of violence, as indicated by national homicide rates, are currently at least four times greater in the U.S. than in these other countries. And that's relatively *good* news: in the early 1990s, this gap was as much as seven times larger.

These patterns represent lethal violence in U.S. society overall, but they mask enormous disparities by race, and the U.S. has a long and troubled history there, too. How have overall levels of violence and differences across racial groups changed over time? The answers are most reliably found in data from death certificates collected by the Centers for

Disease Control and Prevention (CDC). Looking over the data from the last four decades, we can see the entire U.S. homicide victimization rate divided by race. The extraordinary toll of serious violence on the black community is readily apparent.

From 1970 through the early 1990s, the total homicide rate for all U.S. citizens hovered around 10 per 100,000. Since 1993, the rate has declined steadily. In 2010, it was down to just over 5 per 100,000—a "crime drop" phenomenon that has been widely publicized. The trends for blacks and whites largely mirror this pattern; homicide victimization rates have fallen for both groups. But the absolute levels are sharply divergent.

U.S. Homicide Rates, by Race, 1970-2010

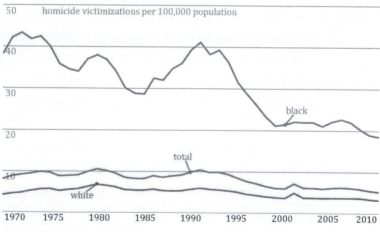

Sources: CDC/NCHS National Vital Statistics System (Mortality) and U.S. Census Bureau.

White rates have always been below 7 and have now fallen to a historic low of 3 per 100,000. In contrast, blacks experience homicide victimization at six to seven times the rates of whites. Even more dramatically, between 1985 and 1993, black homicide deaths rose sharply, an increase attributed by many to the crack epidemic and the presence of guns in the hands of young people in U.S. cities. Other non-lethal but violent crimes reveal similar patterns over time and by race.

Black males suffer from the highest levels of violence overall, but the picture is worse for *young* black males. At its peak, the black male homicide rate was over 70 per 100,000,

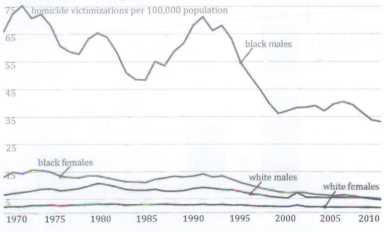

U.S. Homicide Rates, by Race and Sex, 1970-2010

homicide victimizations per 100,000 population

black males

black females

white males

white females

Sources: CDC/NCHS National Vital Statistics System (Mortality) and U.S. Census Bureau.

while the rate was two to three times higher for young black men. In the figure below, we display the homicide victimization rates for young males and females of different racial-ethnic backgrounds in 2010 to illustrate the unique burden of violence borne by young black men.

Even now, when overall murder rates are at their lowest level in 40 years, the homicide victimization rate for black men ages 15 to 34 exceeds 80 per 100,000. This is more than double the rate for non-Hispanic American Indian men, nearly four and a half times that for young Hispanic men, and more than

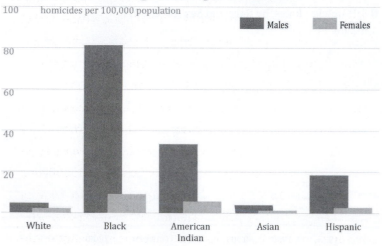

U.S. Homicide Rates among Persons Ages 15-34, 2010

Sources: CDC/NCHS National Vital Statistics System (Mortality) and U.S. Census Bureau.

17 times that for young non-Hispanic white and Asian men. As a result, murder is the leading cause of death among young black males. Their likelihood of being murdered has real implications for black males' life expectancy.

By contrast, the leading cause of death for both young white and Hispanic men is accidental death, followed by suicide for whites and homicide for Hispanics. Females are less likely than males to be homicide victims, regardless of race-ethnicity, but the gender differential is much larger for blacks overall and among young adults.

Leading explanations for the "homicide divide" emphasize how the high levels of economic disadvantage present in segregated black communities increase social and economic isolation. That is, poverty is believed to diminish the resources that hold communities together and keep crime at bay. Thus, heightened rates of lethal violence against blacks are not due to greater individual tendencies toward violence; rather, these deaths are the product of socioeconomic disadvantage and societal racism. High rates of incarceration that are particularly concentrated in black and other minority neighborhoods exacerbate these problems by straining families and destabilizing communities. To overcome the prevalence of violent death in the black community will take nothing short of national-level change, including new approaches to income inequality, segregation, and the disproportionate incarceration of minorities.

asian american exceptionalism and "stereotype promise"

JENNIFER LEE

Jeremy Lin was #1 on *Time* magazine's "100 Most Influential People in the World" list in 2012. As one of only a few Asian American players in the history of the NBA, the first American-born player of Chinese descent, and the first Harvard graduate to play in the league in almost 60 years, Lin has tackled many firsts and, in the process, has broken barriers. Lin splashed onto our screens in February of 2012 when he led the Knicks to an improbable and fantastic winning streak, generating the global phenomenon "Linsanity."

As an unequivocal fan of Jeremy Lin, I was delighted by *Time*'s choice, but I can't help but feel uneasy and ambivalent about the way the magazine described Lin's route to success. The story says Lin achieved success the "old-fashioned way": through hard work, humility, discipline, grit, integrity, and living and playing "the right way." Undoubtedly, Lin works hard and is disciplined; one only needs to view his workout and training video for confirmation.

But what stands out to me is that the attributes and values used to describe Jeremy Lin's success have also been used to describe Asian Americans' academic achievement. Now, the cultural values of hard work, grit, and perseverance are being inscribed into the new territory of sports. This happened without raising eyebrows, because there was a ready-made "success frame" for Asian Americans in education, which was easily transferred to other domains and easily embraced by popular culture.

In earlier writing, I have illustrated how second-generation Chinese and Vietnamese students attain high academic outcomes, even in spite of their disadvantaged class backgrounds. Chinese and Vietnamese immigrant parents and their children construct a narrow "success frame," which is supported by ethnic resources that cut vertically across class lines, thereby making them available to both middle- and working-class ethnics. This helps to explain how the children of immigrants whose parents have only an elementary school education, do not speak English, and work in ethnic restaurants and factories graduate as high school valedictorians, earn admission into the most competitive colleges, and pursue prestigious careers.

Here, I bridge the research in culture and social psychology in a useful way to provide the flip-side explanation; I illustrate how the success frame is validated and reinscribed in institutional contexts, such as schools, by those who presume that Asians are smart, disciplined, and high-achieving. While Claude Steele and his colleagues have found that African American students can suffer from "stereotype threat" (which depresses performance), I find that Asian American students can benefit from what I call a "stereotype promise"— the promise of being viewed through the lens of a positive stereotype, which can boost performance. These social psychological processes can result in what sociologist Robert K. Merton coined a "self-fulfilling prophecy." Consequently, Asian American students—regardless of ethnicity, class, gender, and generational status—gain an advantage over their non-Asian peers in gateway institutions like schools.

asian american symbolic capital

Pierre Bourdieu describes how different forms of capital (economic, cultural, and symbolic) accrue rewards, and by symbolic capital, Bourdieu refers to the resources available to an individual based on prestige or honor. In the context of U.S. schools, Asian American students' symbolic capital benefits them in the way that their teachers perceive, treat, and grade them. The 1.5- and second-generation Chinese and Vietnamese respondents with whom we spoke consistently explained that teachers and school administrators assumed Asian students—regardless of ethnicity, class, or gender—were smart, hard-working, and high-achieving, and, importantly, they explained how these perceptions had very real consequences.

For example, when our research team asked David, a 38-year-old, 1.5-generation Chinese male who now works for Microsoft, whether teachers made assumptions about his academic ability, he answered, "I think positively, just because [of] the perception that Asians, Chinese typically do better in school than the Hispanics and the Caucasians and African Americans."

Similarly, when we asked Julia, a 23-year-old, 1.5-generation Vietnamese who recently graduated from a University of California school the same question, she initially responded, "Oh, actually, I don't know." But after a pause, she continued, "I think just because I was Asian, I think they grouped me in that way. Because even now, when I visit the teachers, they said that we were the best in class. Because all of the Asians at our school, you know, they did well, and we broke academic records and all that."

Both David and Julia recognize that they benefited from their racial status because the top students in their high schools were Asian, generating teachers' perceptions that all Asian students are academically exceptional and outperform their non-Asian peers, including native-born whites.

Their comments offer another important insight: that Asian Americans are compared not only to other racial/ethnic minority groups, but also to native-born whites, signals the need to move beyond the "model minority" thesis—a divisive trope that pits one racial/ethnic minority group against another (typically Asian Americans against African Americans or Latinos).

the consequences of symbolic capital

The symbolic capital afforded to Asian students has real consequences; teachers' positive perceptions affect the grades these students receive, the extra help they are offered with coursework and college applications, and their likelihood of being placed into competitive programs like GATE (Gifted and Talented Education) and into academic tracks like Advanced Placement (AP) and Honors. This appears to be especially the case when Asian students attend racially diverse schools in which Asians are a numerical minority.

Robert's case is illustrative. Robert is a 36-year-old who was born in Taiwan, migrated to the United States at the age of seven, and entered the second grade without speaking a word of English. However, by the third grade, he was placed into GATE. Initially skeptical, we inquired how this happened:

Interviewer: How did you get into GATE? I mean, you came here in second grade and knew no English.

Robert: They tested me, and at first they put me in ESL (English as a second language), and I was like, "Why am I in ESL?" Then somebody tested me again, and they said, "Well, he's really smart." I didn't know what they were talking about.

Interviewer: Do you think your teachers made assumptions about your academic ability based on your ethnic background?

Robert: A lot of them thought because I was Asian—because I was one of the few Asians in my classes and stuff—they would think, "Oh well, he's Asian, he must be smart," or something like that. In elementary school, I was the only Asian in my class. In my whole school I think there were only two or three Asians.

What is remarkable about Robert's placement is that he admitted that after the results of his initial test, the teachers placed him into the ESL track, but upon his mother's insistence, he was re-tested and placed into GATE. Robert recognizes that teachers made positive assumptions about his academic ability not only because he is Asian, but also because he was one of only two or three Asians in a predominantly Latino school.

Robert's story is not unique. Many of the 1.5- and second-generation Chinese and Vietnamese respondents we interviewed were placed in the AP track in high school, and even those who were not in AP or Honors classes were aware that this was the goal.

By contrast, relatively few of the 1.5- and second-generation Mexicans we interviewed were placed into competitive academic tracks, and many were not even sure whether AP or Honors classes had been offered in their schools. Hence, even when Chinese, Vietnamese, and Mexican students attend the same school, they can have vastly different educational experiences because of the segregation that results from academic tracking.

While some of the Chinese and Vietnamese respondents recalled that they successfully tested into the AP or Honors track, others did not remember taking an AP exam, and still others admitted that their junior high grades were not stellar, yet they were placed in high school AP courses nevertheless.

For example, Trang, a 24-year-old, second-generation Vietnamese woman, was placed into Honors classes in high school though she admits that she was not an outstanding junior high student; in fact, she recalls receiving As, Bs, and Cs in her classes. Even more surprising is that Trang has no idea why or how she was placed in Honors classes:

Trang: I think I just got tracked in actually because I don't remember being in any Honors classes in junior high. And they just kind of put me into Honors, and I'm like, "Okay." And it wasn't bad, so I just kind of stuck with it.

Interviewer: Did you have to take a test or anything?

Trang: I don't think so. I think they just stuck me in there from high school.

Once Trang was placed into the Honors track, she began taking her schoolwork more seriously, spending more time doing her homework, and studying hard for tests to keep up with her high-achieving peers. Trang graduated with a GPA above 4.0 and was admitted to all the University of California schools to which she applied.

Perhaps one of the most egregious cases of the symbolic capital accorded to Asian students is that of Angela, a 23-year-old, second-generation Vietnamese woman who described herself as "not very intelligent" and recalls nearly being held back in the second grade. By her account, "I wasn't an exceptional student; I was a straight C student, whereas my siblings, they were quicker than I was, and they were straight A students."

Despite Angela's mediocre grades, she adopted a success frame that mirrored that of her high-achieving coethnics:

"Most Vietnamese, or just Asian people in general, emphasize academics and want their child to become a doctor or an engineer or pharmacist."

Realizing that a critical step in the success frame is getting into the AP track, Angela took the AP exam at the end of junior high school, but failed. Despite having failed, Angela was placed into the AP track in her predominantly white high school. Once there, something "just clicked," and Angela began to excel in her classes.

When we asked, she elaborated, "I wanted to work hard and prove I was a good student," adding, "I think the competition kind of increases your want to do better." She graduated from high school with a 4.2 GPA and was admitted into a highly competitive pharmacy program.

While it is impossible to know how Trang and Angela's academic performance would have differed had they stayed on the school's "regular track," that they were given the opportunity to meet their potential attests to the advantage that Asian students are accorded in the context of American schools.

a self-fulfilling prophecy

While Angela admitted that she took schoolwork more seriously and that things "just clicked," what is lacking in her explanation is an understanding of the social psychological processes that enhanced her performance. Turning to Merton's classic concept of the self-fulfilling prophecy and the literature in social psychology on stereotypes provides some answers.

A self-fulfilling prophecy begins with a false definition of the situation, evoking a new behavior that makes the original false conception come true. Merton provided a number of illustrative examples of self-fulfilling prophecies in his original 1948 article, including the way in which a student's worrying about failing can lead to failure: "Consider the case of the examination neurosis. Convinced that he is destined to fail, the anxious student devotes more time to worry than to study and then turns in a poor examination."

Merton also elucidated how self-fulfilling prophecies operate at the group level to reproduce educational inequalities:

> [If] the dominant in-group believes that Negroes are inferior, and sees to it that funds for education are not "wasted on these incompetents" and then proclaims as evidence of this inferiority that Negroes have disproportionately "only" one-fifth as many college graduates as whites, one can scarcely be amazed by this transparent bit of social legerdemain.

In both Trang and Angela's cases, self-fulfilling prophecies were at work in that the prophecies under consideration (that all Asians will achieve) are not correct, but only become so when they are favored by teachers' high expectations, resulting in a change in the students' behavior and ultimately a change in their academic outcomes.

Neither student believed at the outset that she was academically exceptional or deserving of being in the AP track (especially Angela, who earned straight Cs in junior high school and failed the AP exam). However, once anointed as exceptional and deserving, both students changed their behavior; they took school more seriously, put more time and effort into their homework, and changed the reference group by which they measured their performance, which resulted in straight As and admission to top colleges.

Critically, because Trang and Angela's outcomes matched their teachers' expectations, the teachers can point to these students' stellar academic achievement as proof of their initial assessment about Asian students (that they are smart, high-achieving, and deserving of being placed into the most competitive academic tracks), all the while unmindful of their role in generating a self-fulfilling prophecy.

stereotype threat and stereotype promise

What about the role of stereotypes and how they affect performance? One only needs to turn to the work of Steele and his colleagues for answers.

Steele and his colleagues have found ample evidence of "stereotype threat" in test-taking situations—the threat or the fear of performing in a certain way that would inadvertently confirm a negative stereotype of one's group, which, in turn, depresses performance. Through various social psychological experiments, they have shown that stereotype threat depresses the performance of high-achieving African American students on difficult verbal tests as well as accomplished female math students on difficult math tests when these tests are presented as a measure of ability. They have also shown that performance improves dramatically when the "threat" is lifted—that is, when the tests are presented as problem-solving exercises rather than a measure of ability.

Building on the work of stereotype threat, social psychologist Margaret Shih and her colleagues have found that Asian American females who are strong in math performed better on a math test when their ethnic identity was cued and performed worse when their gender was cued (by cueing, researchers gave students questionnaires prior to taking the tests, which evoked either their gender or racial identities). They conclude that test performance is both malleable and susceptible to implicit cues—what they refer to as "stereotype susceptibility."

Building on this literature, I conceived of "stereotype promise": the promise of being viewed through the lens of a positive stereotype that leads one to perform in such a way that confirms the positive stereotype, thereby enhancing performance. Stereotype promise focuses more broadly on the way in which positive stereotypes can boost performance outside of controlled test-taking environments and in real world settings such as schools and workplaces. Like stereotype threat, the relationship between stereotype promise and performance may be mediated by some of the same mechanisms—anxiety and overcompensating with excess effort—but produce the reverse outcome. Other mechanisms may differ: optimistic rather than pessimistic thoughts, and high rather than low expectations.

In Trang and Angela's cases, once they were placed in a more challenging setting, where teachers' expectations and peer performance were elevated, they benefited from stereotype promise that resulted in their enhanced performance. Angela, in particular, admitted to feeling more anxious about keeping up with her high-achieving peers, overcompensating with more effort, and raising her expectations to match those of her teachers and peers. Stereotype promise is the social psychological process through which Trang and Angela's exceptional academic outcomes became a self-fulfilling prophecy.

What sets stereotype promise apart from the Pygmalion effect (Robert Rosenthal and Lenore Jacobson's finding that teachers' expectations can influence students' performance) is that in their study, teachers were told that certain students (who were selected at random) were "special" and had "intellectual competencies that would in due course be revealed." After one year of the experiment, the researchers found that a higher percentage of "special" students increased their IQ by 20 points or more compared with the control group (47% vs. 19%, respectively). However, unlike in Rosenthal and Jacobson's study, neither Trang nor Angela's teachers were told that these students had "intellectual competencies that would in due course be revealed"; instead, teachers made assumptions about Trang and Angela's academic ability based on group-based stereotypes of Asians.

Indeed, some Asian American academic outcomes are exceptional, but it is not because Asians are superior in some intrinsic sense. Teachers' positive stereotypes of Asian students can change the behavior of even some of the most mediocre pupils, thereby constructing "Asian American exceptionalism" and reinforcing the belief that Asians are intrinsically brighter and more hard-working and place more value on education than other groups—in short, that they achieve success "the right way."

These examples provide a glimpse into the way social psychological processes operate in gateway institutions like schools and reinforce stereotypes about Asian Americans, which not only affect teachers' assessments of Asian students but also Asian Americans students' assessment of themselves. They also illustrate how inequalities are reproduced at the high end of the educational distribution—which is just as critical, yet has been given far less attention than inequalities at the low end.

the unintended consequences of asian american exceptionalism

While "Asian" is an ethnically and socioeconomically diverse category, the racialization of Asians in the United States elides these differences and, consequently, lower-achieving Asians can benefit from symbolic capital as well as stereotype promise.

Still, it's crucial to point out that the construct of "Asian American exceptionalism" can adversely affect students by placing undue pressure on them to excel academically, resulting in feelings of abject failure if they cannot fit the narrowly defined success frame. And rather than rejecting the construct, Asian Americans are more likely to reject their racial and ethnic identities because they feel like outliers.

Asian American exceptionalism also disadvantages Asian American students during the university admissions process. Sociologists Thomas Espenshade and Alexandria

Radford's study of college admissions shows that Asian Americans need a nearly perfect SAT score (1550) to have the same chance of being accepted into one of the top universities as whites who scored 1410 and African Americans who scored 1100. Moreover, whites were 3 times, Hispanics 6 times, and blacks more than 15 times as likely to be accepted at a U.S. university as Asian Americans with similar academic records, pointing to the "Asian tax" that students must pay to be admitted into the country's elite colleges and graduate schools.

While Espenshade and Radford cannot confirm that Asian students face discrimination in the admissions process, their competitive disadvantage is not unlike the discrimination experienced by Jewish students when Ivy League schools attempted to solve "the Jew problem" by instituting quotas and other class-biased measures to restrict their admission, as Jerome Karabel revealed in *The Chosen*. Beginning in the 1920s, Harvard, Yale, and Princeton began requiring recommendation letters, personal interviews, essays, and descriptions of extracurricular activities, which dissuaded and disadvantaged "the wrong kind" of college applicant. Consequently, these Ivy League schools could shroud their admission process through layers of subjectivity and ultimately decrease the number of Jewish students without overtly discriminating against them.

That Asian students have to earn nearly perfect SAT scores to be admitted into elite colleges at the same rate as others whose scores are significantly lower (including white students) is a sobering reminder that even positive, seemingly benign, or even complimentary stereotypes can still be detrimental.

RECOMMENDED READING

Pierre Bourdieu. 1984. *Distinction: A Social Critique of the Judgment of Taste*, Cambridge, MA: Harvard University Press. A description of various forms of capital (economic, cultural, symbolic) that are privileged and reproduce class inequalities.

Thomas J. Espenshade and Alexandria Walton Radford. 2009. *No Longer Separate, Not Yet Equal: Race and Class in Elite College Admission and Campus Life*, Princeton, NJ: Princeton University Press. A comprehensive study of the ways in which race and class impact the college application and admissions process.

Jerome Karabel. 2006. *The Chosen: The Hidden History of Admission and Exclusion at Harvard, Yale, and Princeton*, New York: Mariner Books. Reveals historically exclusionary admissions policies at Ivy League universities.

Robert K. Merton. 1948. "The Self-Fulfilling Prophecy," *Antioch Review* 8(2):193–210. The classic, foundational work establishing that "public definitions of a situation . . . become an integral part of the situation and thus affect subsequent developments."

Cecilia L. Ridgeway. 2011. *Framed by Gender: How Gender Inequality Persists in the Modern World*, New York: Oxford University Press. A path-breaking study of how the gender frame contributes to the persistence of gender inequality, even in domains that lack a history of gendered hierarchies.

Robert Rosenthal and Lenore Jacobson. 1968. *Pygmalion in the Classroom: Teacher Expectation and Pupils' Intellectual Development*, New York: Holt, Rinehart & Winston. A pioneering study of how teachers' expectations can affect students' academic performance.

Margaret Shih, Todd L. Pittinsky, and Nalini Ambady. 1999. "Stereotype Susceptibility: Identity Salience and Shifts in Quantitative Performance," *Psychological Science* 10(1):80–83. Shows how test performance is malleable and susceptible to stereotype cues.

Claude M. Steele and Joshua Aronson. 1995. "Stereotype Threat and the Intellectual Test Performance of African Americans," *Journal of Personality and Social Psychology* 69(5):797–811. Explains how "stereotype threat" depresses performance among African American students.

TSP tie-in

race is a social construction

Race is not a "given." We imagine that race and racial difference are imprinted in our genes, that certain characteristics are linked with certain races—athletic ability, aptitude for mathematics, susceptibility to certain diseases, for instance. But examination of the human genome in recent decades has shown that, in fact, there are no identifiable genetic differences among racial groups as we commonly define them. In other words, at the genetic level, race does not exist.

Race is what sociologists call a "social construction." Along with reading the chapters in this volume, check out thesocietypages.org/race to watch a W. W. Norton & Company animation narrated by The Society Pages' contributor Dalton Conley. The video succinctly explores the notion that humans *create* race, and, consequently, those differences influence our life experiences. It is easy to see that race is a social construction by comparing how race is understood differently across countries. In the United States, for example, we generally understand people as falling into five main categories: Native American, white, black/African American, Latino/Hispanic, and Asian. But these categories are highly specific to the racial history of the U.S. and mean very little to people outside of this context.

These categories have also changed dramatically over time. For example, who is considered "white" in the U.S. has shifted with each new wave of immigrants. When Irish, Italians, and Jews first immigrated in large numbers, the Anglo-Saxon population already living in the U.S. considered each a separate, nonwhite race. But, these groups eventually *became* white as they were able to increase their economic and social standing. And in the South throughout much of the twentieth century, the category of "black" varied across states depending on how much African ancestry one had. At that time, you could cross a state line and legally become a different race.

Racial boundaries—who is included and excluded from the privileged racial groups—are determined by those in power in any given society. Extreme examples include the genocides against those considered members of an inferior race: Jews in Nazi Germany and indigenous people in the U.S. are prime examples. In each case, the more powerful group constructed the other group as a separate and lesser race. Racial categories, then, have more to do with power disparities than with any fundamental differences between people.

It's difficult for many of us to imagine race as being so fluid that it could change with the passing of a law, an updated Census category, or a dictator's decree. The very fact that this is challenging shows how tightly we hold on to the racial categories we "know." But even a quick examination of racial boundaries over time, across countries, and in our genes shows that race is a social construction.

KIA HEISE

latinos, biculturalism, and the in-between

WENDY ROTH

4

For much of American history, race has been a dichotomous, Black-White* affair where the "one-drop rule" dictated that people with any amount of racial mixture were defined legally and socially as Black. In recent generations, however, with the rise of intermarriage and the entrance of new immigrants from all over the world, American racial categories and conceptions have become much more complicated and contested. Latinos provide a particularly revealing case of the new complexities of race in America.

Persons of Hispanic ancestry have long had mixed racial identities and classifications. The history of Latin America is characterized by the mixing of European colonizers, native Indigenous groups, and Africans brought over as slaves.

*Editors' note: The author prefers to capitalize "Black" and "White" along with other socially constructed racial categories.

As a result, the diverse Latino group includes people who look White, Black, and many mixtures in between. In the mid-twentieth century, it was assumed that as they Americanized, Latinos who looked European would join the White race, while those with visible African ancestry would join the Black race, and others might be seen as Native American. For 50 years, the Census has supported this vision by informing us that Latinos could be classified as White, Black, or "other," but not as a race themselves. "Hispanic" remained an ethnic, not a racial category.

Today, few think twice when a breakdown of races in America includes, among others, the categories Black, White, and Latino. Throughout our media and popular culture—in newspapers, television, social media, and even academic research—we tend to treat Whites, Blacks, and Latinos as if they were mutually exclusive groups. How has this come about, given that the United States has long insisted that "Hispanic" or "Latino" is not a race, but an aspect of ethnicity?

To answer this question, I studied Dominicans and Puerto Ricans, two groups whose members span the traditional Black/White color line. I interviewed 60 Dominican and Puerto Rican migrants in New York City, and another 60 Dominicans and Puerto Ricans who have never migrated out of their countries of origin. We spoke about how they understand and classify their own and other people's races, their perception of races in the mainland United States and their home country, what race means to them, and the migrants' integration experiences. Their interviews revealed that most identify with a new, unified racial category that challenges not only the traditional Black-White dichotomy but also the relationship between race and ethnicity in American society. In other words, the experiences of these groups help us to better understand how immigrants' views of collective identity and the relationship between color and culture are reshaping contemporary American racial classifications.

how dominicans and puerto ricans understand identity and race

My respondents all identified primarily as "Latino," "Dominican," or "Puerto Rican." Even among those who had migrated to New York City, these were strongly held identities, associated with language, culture, and nationhood—the kinds of attitudes, attributes, and claims American scholars tend to associate with ethnicity. But many respondents also gave the same answers when asked specifically how they identified their race. They explained that, with their country's history of racial intermixing over many generations, the meaning of "Puerto Rican" or "Dominican" is itself racialized as the mixture of White, Indigenous, and Black. For instance, Blanca, an arts administrator in Puerto Rico, looks European. Because of her mixed roots, she identifies herself as Puerto Rican.

Many Puerto Ricans consider themselves . . . [a] mixture of blancos, indios and negros. . . . I consider myself a mixture of blanca, negra and maybe india. . . . I don't consider myself mulata because mulato is blanco and negro. I consider myself Puerto Rican, and the Puerto Rican is that.

Puerto Rican is blanco, negro, and indio?

Yes. I don't know if I have indio race and I don't know if I have negro race but if I look at myself in the mirror I think that, although I have, look, straight hair and I'm more blanca than negra, but I'm a Puerto Rican. There is no way that I'm not Latina.

Gregorio, a taxi driver from the Dominican Republic, identifies his race as Dominican.

Could you tell me what race you consider yourself to be?

Well, from the country, I mean, Dominican. Dominican.

Okay. And would you say that Dominican is a race?

Yes, I believe so. Yes, because . . . each country has its race of origin. . . . I'm Dominican and everywhere you go, you say,

"What country [are you] from?" or "What race?" Well, you say, "Dominican."

Regardless of whether African, Indigenous, or European features predominate, Dominicans and Puerto Ricans view "race" as this shared ancestry, not as something that divides them. Puerto Ricans and Dominicans refer to a range of physical appearances as "color," but insist that such appearances—such as blanco, negro, mestizo, trigueño, and a host of others—are not their race. Eduardo, a young Dominican administrative assistant in Santo Domingo, gave a response typical of both groups when he said, "They've taught us that this is color . . . for me, they're only skin colors." Many respondents believe that "color," or appearance, is just a matter of chance—what happens to get expressed—but that a person's racial mixture is latent and can present itself in future generations. For instance, Jaime, a Puerto Rican professor in San Juan, locates the essence of the Puerto Rican race in an ancestral inheritance:

> If . . . you're Puerto Rican, [and] you have the races, Spanish, Indian, and African, then that's your race. And it doesn't matter if you're more blanco, or if this one is more negro, and they got married, the son still has the race. You see? Because the race isn't lost, the pedigree isn't lost, you know, you carry it.

As a result, Jaime maintains, "I don't think that the color defines a race." This view of "Puerto Rican," "Dominican," or even "Latino" as a mixed racial ancestry is quite different from how Americans traditionally think of race and distinguish it from ethnicity.

confronting the american racial context

Studies by scholars such as Laura Gómez and Julie Dowling show that other Latino immigrants, such as Mexicans, have similarly understood their ethnicities as a mixture of races. I found that when my migrant respondents first came to the mainland U.S., they brought this "mixed" understanding of race with them. When early migrants arrived, this view ran up against the prevailing American racial images and categories, especially those associated with darker skin tones.

Most people from the Hispanic Caribbean have some African ancestry, which would have led to them being classified as Black under the United States' one-drop rule. This surprised and often frustrated migrants who identified their race in terms of their nationality. Celia, a Puerto Rican school counselor who was sent to live with her older sister in New York in 1955, explains:

> I discovered so much about racism when I came to this country. . . . When I came to school . . . for my ethnicity, they put

Black. And then my sister went [to correct it] and she said, "She is a Lat—" At that time we didn't use the word "Latino." We said Puerto Rican.

. . . did they change your race on the form?

Yeah, they changed it. . . . I don't think they gave her a hard time. But yet, it was a problem. It was a problem.

The problem, for Celia, was one of respect. Being classified as Black not only imposed a race she did not accept, but also implied a lower status.

Because of their treatment as Black, even where Puerto Ricans and Dominicans have been allowed to live and travel has been constrained. Antonio, a Puerto Rican migrant who arrived in New York in 1947, settled in Spanish Harlem. He became aware of racial divisions through the territorial demarcations that divided his neighborhood landscape:

East Harlem was divided into two portions: the portion east of 3rd Avenue and the portion west of 3rd Avenue. East of 3rd Avenue was where all the Italians lived, and there was a tremendous amount of fights between the kids. And the demilitarized zone was 3rd Avenue because it had an "el," an elevated train. I had to go to the elevated train to go downtown or whatever so that was a place that it was safe to go.

But you wouldn't go past [east of] that and the Italians couldn't go west of that. I was very young when I first became aware of that because we were told "Don't go east of 3rd Avenue or your life is in danger." . . . and then west of that was Central Harlem where all the Blacks were living and we mixed with Blacks.

The African Americans Antonio grew up with could not understand why he did not identify as Black. Having internalized the one-drop rule themselves, they insisted, "If you're mixed, you're Black." This, after all, was their reality.

But much has changed in recent years, led in no small part by the tremendous growth of Latino populations. In New York City, the Puerto Rican population grew from about 600,000 in 1960 to almost 900,000 in 1990. Between 1960 and 2000, the Dominican population grew by more than 3,000% to become the second-largest Latino group in the city. Moreover, the entire Latino population of New York City has surged from less than 10% in 1960 to 27% in 2000 and has become increasingly diverse. With more than one in four New Yorkers identifying as Latino, native-born Americans are more familiar with these populations, and the communities themselves have more power to determine how they will be classified.

Celia, quoted above, now teaches at a school in the center of Spanish Harlem. In her school, Latinos are the majority, and there is no question that staff and administrators are fully sensitive to their cultural backgrounds and unique way of thinking about race, nationalism, and ethnicity. The size and prominence of the population has helped them assert their view of race as based on culture, a view that also fosters a shared Latino identity. And just as "Puerto Rican" or "Dominican" represented the particular mixture of Spanish, African, and Taíno peoples, these migrants have applied their understanding of race to view "Latinos" as a mixed-race group. This is much like José Vasconcelos's notion of a "cosmic race" created out of the blending of peoples in Latin America. In racializing the "Latino" category, many respondents highlight the contrast to European Americans, who historically tried to avoid the racial mixture that characterizes modern Latinos.

Migrant respondents tend to emphasize their Latino identities in situations where they see it as advantageous. Those with darker appearances find it particularly useful to distinguish themselves from Blacks. Yesenia, a retired Puerto Rican garment worker, explained, "Negro [dark-skinned] Puerto Ricans don't want to be Black Americans. . . . When they come in the elevator and you think they are Black Americans and you speak English to them . . . they quickly speak Spanish to you." Speaking Spanish or revealing their name is usually enough for others to "reclassify" those initially "mistaken" for Black.

but not white, either

But by the same token, those with lighter appearances often find that Americans do not accept them as White. When they assert a White identity, an identity many held in their countries of origin, light-skinned Latinos are often corrected by people around them. Carla, a Dominican lawyer, learned that she is no longer considered White through an experience at college.

> In my country, I'm very light in color. That is, very, very light among Dominicans. I even think that my personal identification card . . . said White. And actually I considered myself White before, until I came here. And later when I arrived here I realized that no, that I'm not White and that actually I realized what discrimination was, that is, being treated differently.

> *And how did you realize that you . . . aren't White?*

> That happened one day when we were at the university, my friend and me. My friend is also Dominican and she is negra. We were studying at the university until very, very late [so we were told to call] the security office and ask them to accompany us to our home. . . . So I called, and they asked me how

we looked . . . I told them that we were two women and that one was Black and the other one White. And my friend who had lived in the U.S. for some time laughed and she told me, "Do you think that you're White?"

Through reminders like these, light-skinned migrants learn that the most privileged racial category is the hardest to join. Either through their own efforts to move up the racial hierarchy or other people's efforts to keep them down, Latinos of all appearances find themselves occupying a middle rung on the country's racial ladder.

Of course, light-skinned Latinos could become White by integrating culturally—losing their accent, language, and Latino identity. But many of the migrants I spoke with did not. In addition to being proud of their roots, they also saw distinct advantages to being bilingual and bicultural in a country with a growing Latino community. Nilda has light skin and could pass for a White American, but when applying for jobs she finds that it helps to be seen as a Puerto Rican English speaker. Even if her English is not perfect, her ability to speak Spanish lifts her above other job candidates, especially in customer service.

Migrants of all appearances recognize the tremendous potential of being able to "navigate in two worlds" as the Latino community (and market) grows, which makes them reluctant to fully "Americanize." Even for those who are largely acculturated, the prominence of the Latino community in New York City's psyche keeps the identity alive. Subtle indications of their origins—their names, references to their family roots—remind others that they are part of this group. Unlike an ethnicity, the Latino race does not seem to be fading over time.

immigration, integration, and race and ethnicity

In August 2012, the Census Bureau announced that it is considering replacing the separate race and Hispanic origin questions with one combined question that will place "Latino" on equal footing with other recognized race categories. In recent censuses, about 40% of Latinos have chosen not to select White, Black, or one of the other races listed and have instead marked themselves as "Other" race. Many interpret this to mean that they identify their race as Latino or as their nationality.

But will being seen and now counted as a race affect Latinos' place in the American social hierarchy and their opportunities for empowerment? In her book *In the Shadow of Race*, Victoria Hattam suggests that U.S. groups that have been viewed as ethnicities have experienced more social mobility over time while those viewed as races are often relegated to the bottom of society. In effect, she suggests that there are some real costs to being seen in racial terms.

However, most of the groups that were defined as ethnicities and experienced mobility in the past were European, a category that was already, in effect, racialized and associated with Whiteness. They tended to lose their primary attachment to their ethnicity as they acculturated and were able to position themselves as part of the White race. This has always been far harder for those with African ancestry, who are unlikely to be seen as White no matter how integrated they are.

It has also been difficult for groups to shed a strong ethnic identity when they experience ongoing immigration, as sociologist Tomás Jiménez has shown. A steady stream of newcomers ties the group to its immigrant origins in the public mind. In this sense, Latin Americans are different from earlier European immigrants. The Depression and World War II spurred decades with little immigration, when European groups could shed their immigrant identities. But steady Latin American immigration over the last 50 years has produced an association between our images of "Latino" and "newcomer." Latinos are in a unique position relative to other immigrant groups, past and present. Some members of the group—those with light skin and Americanized behavior—

could have followed the path of earlier groups toward Whiteness even if it meant changing their names or hiding their origins. But other members—actual newcomers and those with darker skin—influenced public perceptions of the group overall.

The fact that Latinos have not, by and large, shed their Latino identities also creates advantages for the group as a whole. Groups that identify their shared interests and structural barriers are more likely to be involved in political mobilization. Yen Le Espiritu has shown this to be the case among Asian Americans who have fostered a sense of Asian panethnicity with common structural positions and shared interests that stem from their racialized treatment. A Latino identity functions in a similar way. The attention given to Latinos in the 2012 election cycle shows their ability to mobilize as a voting bloc, and Latinos will likely only continue to use their numbers for political gain.

The intertwining of race and ethnicity in the national imagination has created greater solidarity within the group. That can improve the situation of all Latinos rather than the lucky few. A common racial identity allows those with lighter skin and greater advantages to share resources and information with those with darker skin. In other words, the Latino race, whether embraced or imposed, might help to lift the entire group and not just those members who are able to jump across the color line into Whiteness. As they form a strong political voting bloc and gain the ability to self-identify on official documents like Census forms, American Latinos will continue to further express their identity and challenge the ways Americans have traditionally thought about race and ethnicity.

RECOMMENDED READING

Julie A. Dowling. Forthcoming 2014. *On the Borders of Identity: Mexican Americans and the Question of Race*, Austin: University of Texas Press. This study examines Mexican American responses to the Census race question and explores the disjuncture between federal definitions and local constructions of race.

Yen Le Espiritu. 1992. *Asian American Panethnicity: Bridging Institutions and Identities*, Philadelphia, PA: Temple University Press. A case study of how diverse national-origin groups can come together as a new panethnic group.

Laura E. Gómez. 2007. *Manifest Destinies: The Making of the Mexican American Race*, New York: New York University Press. Uses New Mexico as a case study to explore the paradox of Mexican Americans' legal designation as White but social position as non-White.

Victoria Hattam. 2007. *In the Shadow of Race: Jews, Latinos, and Immigrant Politics in the United States*, Chicago, IL: University of Chicago Press. A comprehensive study revealing how the assignation of certain groups as ethnicities has reinforced the racial inequality of other groups.

Tomás R. Jiménez. 2010. *Replenished Ethnicity: Mexican Americans, Immigration and Identity*, Berkeley: University of California Press. A cleverly designed study that examines the role of continued immigration on later-generation Mexican Americans' identity and experiences.

Clara E. Rodríguez. 2000. *Changing Race: Latinos, the Census, and the History of Ethnicity in the United States*, New York: New York University Press. Uses historical analysis, personal interviews, and Census data to show that Latino identity is fluid, situation dependent, and constantly changing.

David R. Roediger. 2005. *Working Toward Whiteness: How America's Immigrants Became White: The Strange Journey from Ellis Island to the Suburbs*, New York: Basic Books. Roediger shows how American ethnic groups—like Jewish, Italian, and Polish Americans—came to be seen as White only after immigration laws became more restrictive in the 1920s and 1930s.

beyond the big, bad racist: shared meanings of white identity and supremacy

MATTHEW W. HUGHEY

Western societies possess a fetish for the conflict between polar opposites. And when it comes to the "hot button" topic of race, these opposites seem all the more useful. We often make meaning and sense of racial conflict by searching for the quintessentially "good" and "evil" people involved.

Such lumping and splitting is nothing new. Scholars have long noted the framing of absolute rights and wrongs when it comes to racial identity and racism. Sociologist Jack Niemonen remarked in 2007 that we often "paint a picture of social reality in which battle lines are drawn, the enemy identified, and the victims sympathetically portrayed, . . .

[distinguishing] between 'good' whites and 'bad' whites."
Sociologist Eduardo Bonilla-Silva believes scholars can also impose their worldview in their evaluation of data, as he wrote in 2010: "Hunting for 'racists' is the sport of choice of those who practice the 'clinical approach' to race relations— the careful separation of good and bad, tolerant and intolerant Americans." For his part, journalist Tim Wise chimed in after Barack Obama's first presidential victory, writing, "While it may be tempting . . . to seek to create a dichotomy whereby the 'bad whites' are the ones who voted against the black guy, while the 'good whites' are the ones who voted for him, such a dualism is more than a little simplistic."

The racist/antiracist pairing is partially due to the dissemination of simplistic explanations about racism. For example, in his 1949 piece "Discrimination and National Welfare," the sociologist Robert K. Merton advanced a theory of racial prejudice and discrimination. Merton argued that prejudice and discrimination were two separate forms of racial animus, and were themselves dichotomous variables. This theory permitted four "types" of white people: the "All-Weather Liberal" (the unprejudiced non-discriminator), the "Fair-Weather Liberal" (the unprejudiced discriminator), the "Fair-Weather Illiberal" (the prejudiced non-discriminator), and the "All-Weather Illiberal" (the prejudiced discriminator). In this scheme, one could be prejudiced without discriminating (e.g., a white manager who *believes* African Americans are inferior employees, but still treats people equally) or discriminate without a prejudicial belief in racial inferiority (e.g., the white manager who *believes* in racial equality but refuses to hire African Americans for fear of white customers' reprisal).

Such parsing out of the good whites (the All-Weather Liberal) and the bad whites (the All-Weather Illiberal) has saturated our culture and has turned many a layperson into a self-professed race expert. In this model, racism belongs to the realm of either behavior (discrimination) or thoughts (prejudice) and manifests as little more than a person choosing racism or being coerced into it. With this understanding, we can divide the world into those whites who are "sick" with this disease and those who are the "healthy" anti- or nonracist white people.

Let's look at a few examples. *CBS News* reported that, when actor Michael Richards (of Kramer fame on the series *Seinfeld*) repeatedly yelled, "He's a nigger!" at a black heckler during a 2009 comedy show, many were unsure what to make of his comments. In part because Richards does not comport with the commonly shared expectations of who a "racist" is and what a "racist" looks like, he was able to cool the flames. He visited CBS, on their national newscast, to state: "I'm not a racist. . . . That's what's so insane."

In 2008, MSNBC reported that Geraldine Ferraro (former congresswoman and vice presidential candidate) had remarked that the only reason Barack Obama is successful at politics is because of his race. (Twenty years earlier Ferraro made a similar remark about Jesse Jackson, stating in the *Washington Post* that if he was "not black, he wouldn't be in the race.") As controversy erupted, Ferraro insisted in a *Boston Globe* op-ed that her comments had not been racist and that *she* was the victim of racism: "If you're white you can't open your mouth without being accused of being racist." Soon, the story fell out of the news cycle.

And when *People* reported that Duane "Dog" Chapman (of *Dog the Bounty Hunter* acclaim) had been recorded calling his son's then-girlfriend (who is black) a "nigger," many pounced. But apologizing on his behalf, another of his sons responded on *Hannity and Colmes*: "My dad is not a racist man. If he was, he would have no hair. He'd have swastikas on his body and he would go around talking about Hitler. That's what a racist is to me." Again, after a cursory explanation, the controversy faded away.

The responses from Richards, Ferraro, and Chapman largely resonate with the American mainstream because of the already established notions of racism and antiracism; we easily draw boundaries between supposedly "good" and "bad" whites because one group is ostensibly easily recognizable.

That is, the white "racists" of our culture are supposed to be the fringe, radical bad apples. They wear hoods and swastikas, fly the Confederate flag, or talk about their desire for a segregated nation. Anything less than this cartoon can't possibly be racist.

This fairy-tale explanation simply will not do. It fails to acknowledge or explain how understandings of the natural or cultural dysfunctions among people of color are widespread and even accepted as what Eduardo Bonilla-Silva called, in 2010, "common sense." This does not account for how, as Edward Glaeser and Jacob Vigdor found in 2012, the average white lives in a 78% white neighborhood. This model does not address why the median wealth of white households is 20 times that of black households and 18 times that of Hispanic households, as reported by Rajesh Kochhar and his colleagues in 2011. It cannot tell us why the Center for Constitutional Rights found in 2012 that whites are much less likely to be racially profiled and arrested than people of color. And this paradigm certainly fails to explain why, in studies like Devah Pager's 2003 research, whites *with* criminal records receive more favorable treatment in the search for employment than blacks *without* criminal records.

Simply put, this approach fails to get us beyond the big, bad "racist." It cannot account for white supremacy within our discourse, neighborhoods, wealth accumulation, criminal justice system, and labor markets. By throwing the label of "racist" at one individual or group at the expense of another (e.g., "They are racists, but we are not"), we treat racism as atypical instead of systemic. We fail to fix our attention on the normal and benign social relations that reproduce racial inequities and white dominance.

In my own research, published in my 2012 book *White Bound: Nationalists, Antiracists, and the Shared Meanings of Race*, I find an eerie resemblance between how the "bad whites" (a white nationalist organization) and the "good whites" (a white antiracist group) make meaning of race and white racial identity. But don't get me wrong. Both groups pose different kinds of threats and promises, and there remain deep differences between white nationalists (not to mention within that "movement"—it's a heterogeneous bunch, as Leonard Zeskind and Eileen O'Brien have found) and white antiracists (they, too, are diffuse and varied).

In over 14 months of ethnography, I examined how both groups held analogous and commonsense "ideals" of white identity that functioned as seemingly neutral yardsticks against which cultural behavior, norms, values, and expectations were measured. In any given setting or context, I saw how an ideal of whiteness emerged alongside many other ways of "being white" that were complicit, subordinate, or marginalized in relation to that ideal.

I found that a shared idea of white racial identity—what I call "hegemonic whiteness"—extended beyond the overt political goals and racialized agendas of both groups. Members of both groups valorized certain performances of whiteness that they strove to attain but of which many fell short. This resulted in a great deal of variation in white racial identities, but it was a variation cohesively bound by shared understandings and expectations.

This approach differs from the paradigms of both Bonilla-Silva's "color-blind racism" and what Lawrence Bobo and Ryan Smith called, in 1998, *"laissez-faire* racism." Both theories illustrate how the racial outlooks of white Americans have shifted from overtly racist "Jim Crow" attitudes—which endorsed segregation, advocated for legal discrimination, and embraced the belief that nonwhites held biological deficiencies—to a more subtle racism based on the beliefs in natural differences among racial groups, cultural-based pathologies of nonwhite people, and a decline in racial inequality. Together, these attitudes and ideologies rationalize racial oppression in the United States.

Rather than concentrate on racialized attitudes or ideologies, I center on the processes of identity formation as causal mechanisms that reproduce racial inequality. That is, when the routine ways white people do things together are interpreted not just as deviant or exceptional *actions* but as marking their immoral, dysfunctional, or superior *identity*, then the mechanisms that reproduce an unequal society exist in the very meanings of our identities—in the very ways we go about (re)accomplishing our sense of self. How we then go about making meaning of race is not simply an exercise in interpretation; it is the heart that circulates our social life-blood. It is the brick and mortar of our social structures.

In the groups I studied, the processes of meaning-making and social expectations were neither written in stone nor one-dimensional. How they were redrawn or emphasized depended on specific situations. Among both white nationalists and white antiracists, I found an ideal or hegemonic white identity was often defined in relation to people of color and their supposedly "dysfunctional" pathologies, by whites claiming an embattled victim status, by framing themselves as a kind of messianic "white savior" to people of color, in objectifying nonwhite people or products as essentially "cool" or "exotic" and using that "color capital" to credentialize the self, and by exhibiting entitlement to racialized knowledge.

These dimensions are not static traits of whiteness, such as "invisibility" (that is, how, compared to nonwhites, whites are able to attach less importance to their racial identity and culture) or "individualistic color blindness" (how, compared to nonwhites, whites are more likely to embrace individualism and less likely to adhere to color-blind ideals). While

Douglas Hartmann, Joseph Gerteis, and Paul R. Croll found that, in 2009, roughly 15% of whites demonstrated uniform adherence to such beliefs, I demonstrate in *White Bound* how whites from across the political spectrum emphasized any one of the above five dimensions within specific social relations.

When I say "social relations," I refer to situations in which people make sense of themselves in relation to others so as to comprehend the situation and act accordingly. For example, children might realize their expected subordinated identity in relation to a parent and act accordingly (consciously or unconsciously) to receive praise and status as either a "normal" or "good" child. Conversely, they may rebel, then navigate the consequences of explicit punishment and implicit judgment. Even when people act alone, social relations are at work when they imagine how others will evaluate them and their actions.

When you start to look at white racism this way, the everyday use of racist meanings as a basic resource for structuring social relations is clearly widespread. These meanings are not confined to explicit discussions or encounters associated with racial identity or race relations. Rather, the racially segregated and hierarchical character of American life normalizes racist meanings amid an array of whites across the spectrum.

I found a pattern in which members of both the white nationalists and the white antiracists regularly conceived of their whiteness as bland, boring, or somehow lacking in racial authenticity. I called this shared, intersubjective feeling "white debt." Because of white debt, both sets of activists attempted to control, apprehend, and appropriate people and objects coded as nonwhite. I labeled such objects and people "color capital."

In one instance, "Daniel" (a 32-year-old registered nurse) who had been a member of the white nationalist group National Equality for All (NEA) for four years, explained to me: "Despite my politics, I have quite a few good black friendships." I asked, "So they know you are a member of NEA?" Daniel answered:

> Some do, some don't. I mean we disagree about some things, but who doesn't? But they're good black people; they have jobs, families, are intelligent people. We see each other a lot at the gym. I have lunch at least once a week with one of them. . . . You can't say I'm some redneck, ignorant racist now, can you?

Daniel's interracial ties work like a form of capital that can credential him, particularly among those who would label white nationalists like him "ignorant racists."

Various members of the white antiracist organization I call "Whites for Racial Justice" (WRJ) also evoked such a discourse. "Andre" (a 24-year-old graduate student) stated:

> I really believe in what we are doing, and I think segregation is flat-out wrong, and so, I mean, that's good, you know . . . and I guess outside of WRJ I feel like I earn a bit of respect from others who think that we're just a bunch of crazy radicals. I use the fact that I have two black neighbors to show others that we live what we say; it earns me respect.

What earns you respect?

> Oh, the fact that I have two black neighbors, I get an advantage from it. . . . I mean, I brought [one of his black neighbors] by WRJ the other day, and it was great. He was asking me questions about what we did, and he seemed to look at me in a different light, and to the other guys [in WRJ] I became one of the "good" white people.

After I turned off the audio recorder, Andre further explained that he felt "cool" when he brought his black neighbor to meet his fellow WRJ members; it reminded him of being in elementary school during "show and tell."

In another example, when I asked the white nationalist "Laurence" (a 55-year-old lawyer) why he prominently displayed an extensive CD collection of black jazz, he replied:

Black jazz is not like White jazz. It's carnal and full of emotion. White jazz is more laid back—elevator music like, softer somehow.... Black artists have a soul and a ... [long pause]. I don't know ... they have something underneath the music, it's the rhythm or something.... Maybe it's because of discrimination or whatever ... maybe after a few hundred years of reverse racism then Whites will play jazz like that but I doubt it.... There's a harsh quality to it ... it goes back to Africa and has been passed on genetically. Whites don't have it, so I listen to it. I just like it.

When I noticed a similar phenomenon of almost exclusive ownership of music performed by black artists in the homes of several WRJ members, such as "Blake" (a 22-year-old in retail sales), I was told:

I like hip-hop and jazz mostly, because the music is more real to me. I feel better when I listen to it, like I am more in touch with the human side of me. Even with the more hard-core rap music, I don't like as much of it, but it's like it really hits me here you know [pointing to his heart], it's valid here.

So you like artists like Kenny G. or Eminem?

Get out of here! [laughing] They are jokes, I mean, no . . .
listen. . . . I like it because it's real, it expresses something I
wouldn't be able to get otherwise. I'm not black so I can't
really get it, but I get closer to it when I listen to it, you
know?

*What do you mean by "it" when you say you really can't get
"it"?*

I mean, the black experience, I get closer to it with hip-hop, I
guess that's why I like it. It fits with my whole life and being
in [WRJ].

The equating of black music with soul, carnality, validity,
and realness reveals many of the racist and essentialist features embodied in the very dispositions of WRJ and NEA
members. What might appear as individual choice, psychological disposition, or personal taste is, instead, a patterned
social relation structured by the pursuit of color capital.
The groups I studied wish for a completely different racial
future, but we should take into account that their uses of
color capital served a similar function. They objectified
black and brown bodies in the formation of a more robust
white self.

Research like mine suggests that many whites possess similar and shared definitions of social relations and their identities relative to those situations. Shared understandings of racial categories provide whites with a common knowledge for how to make meaning of their own racial identity and how they should relate to others. Because there are infinite contexts and situations in which people find themselves, the dominant meanings of white racial identity—as a primary social category—provide a way to navigate everyday life regardless of context. Shared understandings of race allow quick responses within the structural constraints of unexpected interactions.

The dimensions of an ideal white racial identity are powerful, implicit, and far-reaching scripts and expectations to which people are socially accountable. While meanings are certainly situational, they are never disconnected from extra-local concerns. Accordingly, Michael Schwalbe and his colleagues wrote in 2000 of a larger "net of accountability," shared with people outside any particular organization or setting.

Further, though people navigate the meanings of race in different ways in different settings, dominant expectations constrain and enable actions in recognizable patterns—an "overarching configuration of practices," Amanda E. Lewis called it in 2004—that produce similar performances of white racial identity.

The far reach of these dimensions provides the net that binds whites to expected actions and creates a multidimensional yet coherent sense of white racial identity. These expectations and accountabilities let whites explain and justify their actions in ways that appear normal and even racially neutral, even as they preserve the privileges and exploitative social relations associated with whiteness.

RECOMMENDED READING

Eduardo Bonilla-Silva. 2010 [2003]. *Racism without Racists: Color-Blind Racism and the Persistence of Racial Inequality in the United States*. Lanham, MD: Rowman & Littlefield. Now in its third edition, this "modern classic" rests on interview data from the 1997 Survey of College Students and the 1998 Detroit Area Study to demonstrate how racist ideology is reproduced without the presence of stereotypical "racists."

Douglas Hartmann, Joseph Gerteis, and Paul R. Croll. 2009. "An Empirical Assessment of Whiteness Theory: Hidden from How Many?" *Social Problems*. 56(3): 403–424. Uses the American Mosaic Project Survey to analyze whether whites actually embrace the core theoretical tenets of white racial identity: the conflation of whiteness with invisibility (or normality), the ignorance of white racial privileges, and adherence to individualistic, color-blind ideals.

Matthew W. Hughey. 2012. "Stigma Allure and White Antiracist Identity Management," *Social Psychology Quarterly*. 75(3): 219–241. Examines why many white antiracists embrace a broken and spoiled *white* and *antiracist* identity that enables claims of moral commitment and political authenticity.

Amanda E. Lewis. 2004. "What Group? Studying Whites and Whiteness in the Era of Colorblindness," *Sociological Theory*. 22(4): 623–646. Highlights the three distinct challenges of studying white racial identity and advances the question of "hegemonic whiteness" that my own book, *White Bound*, attempts to answer.

Leonard Zeskind. 2009. *Blood and Politics: The History of the White Nationalist Movement from the Margins to the Mainstream*. New York: Farrar Straus and Giroux. The most comprehensive study of the modern white supremacist movement and the major figures within these organizations.

cultural contexts

white trash: the social origins of a stigmatype

MATT WRAY

6

White trash. For many, the name evokes images of trailer parks, meth labs, beat-up Camaros on cinder blocks, and poor rural folks with too many kids and not enough government cheese. It's a put-down, the name given to those whites who don't make it, either because they're too lazy or too stupid. Or maybe it's because something's wrong with their inbred genes. Whatever the reason, it's their own damn fault they live like that.

On the other hand, there are plenty of people now willing to wear "white trash" as a badge of honor. Much as African American youth turned the despised word *nigger* into an expression of pride and solidarity (usually as the abbreviated *nigga*) or the way that LGBT activists have reclaimed *queer*, some white people now identify as *white trash* to signal rebelliousness and cultural difference—their refusal of a bland, mainstream white society that oppresses and stifles.

And there is a third popular use of the term: to denigrate and punish the rich and famous when they act badly. Despite her millions, Paris Hilton can be called out for a "trashy" lifestyle, and George Clooney can tell us, in his self-mocking kind of way, that beneath a dapper exterior, he's really just white trash. And, as comedian and actor Tom Arnold said of his marriage to comedian, actress, and sometime political aspirant Roseanne Barr, "We're America's worst nightmare—white trash with money!"

So, is *white trash*, as campy director John Waters once said, "the last racist thing you can say and get away with"? Or has it become a symbol of something like ethnic pride? Or is it just a comical phrase used to condemn, excuse, or celebrate bad behavior, like too much drinking, cussing, fighting, and general screwing around?

And then there's the bigger question: why should we care, anyway? What makes white trash talk anything more than pop culture trivia? To answer these questions it helps to look to the past, to see when and how the term arose, and to think about the uses to which it has been put, by whom, and why. Surprisingly, the answers have a lot to do with our changing ideas about sex, class, and gender.

what did you call me?

Whether they say "white trash" or not, most Americans are unaware of its long and ugly history. Pressed to venture a guess, you'd probably say that the term arose in the Deep South, some time in the middle of last century, as a term that whites coined to demean other whites less fortunate than themselves. Try again.

The term *white trash* dates back not to the 1950s but to the *1820*s. It arose not in Mississippi or Alabama, but in and around Baltimore, Maryland. The best guess is that it was invented not by whites but by African Americans (both free and enslaved) as a term of abuse—to disparage local poor whites. Some would have been newly arrived Irish immigrants, others semi-skilled workers drawn to jobs in the post-Revolution building boom. Still other trashy types may have been white servants, waged or indentured, working in the homes and estates of area elites. As it does today, the term registered contempt and disgust, and it suggested sharp hostilities among social groups essentially competing for the same resources—the same jobs, the same opportunities, and even the same marriage partners.

But if *white trash* originated in African American slang, it was middle-class and elite whites who found the term most compelling and useful—and ultimately, this is the crowd that made it part of popular American speech.

Over the next 40 years, the phrase began to appear more and more frequently in the printed materials of more privileged white readers. In 1854 Harriet Beecher Stowe, in her bestselling *Key to Uncle Tom's Cabin*, devoted an entire chapter to "Poor White Trash," explaining that the slave system "produced not only heathenish, degraded, miserable slaves, but it produces a class of white people who are, by universal admission, more heathenish, degraded, and miserable." The degradation was due, Stowe argued, to the way plantation slavery locked up productive soil in the hands of a few large planters, leaving ordinary white people to struggle for subsistence. But there were other factors as well:

> Without schools or churches, these miserable families grow up heathen on a Christian soil, in idleness, vice, dirt, and discomfort of all sorts. They are the pest of the neighborhood, the scoff and contempt or pity even of the slaves. The expressive phrase, so common in the mouths of the negroes, of "poor white trash," says all for this luckless race of beings that can be said.

Southern secessionists and proslavery apologists countered that it wasn't the lack of access to good farmland, compulsory education, or religious influence that made poor white trash so worthy of contempt. In their view, the depravity of white trash sprung from the "tainted blood" that ran through their veins. As one educated Southerner averred on the eve of the Civil War:

> Everywhere, North and South, in Maine or Texas, in Virginia or New-York, they are one and the same; and have undoubtedly had one and the same origin, namely, the poor-houses and prison-cells of Great Britain. Hence we again affirm . . . that there is a great deal more in blood than people in the United States are generally inclined to believe.

Poor white depravity wasn't attributable to any economic or social system—it was inherited, a pre-Revolutionary legacy.

taking out the trash

By the 1890s, America's burgeoning eugenics movement got hold of this idea and never let go. Most Americans are well aware of the horrors of Nazi eugenics—the early- and mid-nineteenth-century idea that through proper breeding techniques and controlling the fertility of the "unfit," one could produce a superior race. But few care to remember that Nazi eugenicists were taking their cues from American predecessors, who, beginning in the early decades of the twentieth century, had successfully lobbied for laws permitting states to involuntarily sterilize people considered unsuited for sexual reproduction.

While many American eugenicists railed about the threats posed by hordes of "dysgenic" immigrants (nonwhite, often, but also people from "undesirable" countries and bloodlines of all sorts), the core of eugenical science was based in field studies of poor rural whites. These studies of poor white families and kinship networks were carried out all over the East and Midwest, from upstate New York to Virginia to Ohio. Authors gave their subjects colorful names like the Jukes, the Kallikaks, the Happy Hickories, and the Smoky Pilgrims. They documented a high incidence of criminality and violence among the men and increased promiscuity and fecundity among the women.

White trash was a threat, in other words, because these people were both unfit for reproduction and spectacular at it.

Field researchers often produced evidence they claimed demonstrated the deplorable effects of "defective germ plasm" (what we would today consider genetic material) passed from one generation to the next, sometimes through the immorality of interracial sex, the sexual predations of fathers on their own daughters, or reproduction between close cousins. The last two categories of illicit sexual behavior, grouped under the term *consanguinity*, were put forth again and again, in study after study, as evidence of the need to control the fertility of poor whites, whose incestuous, cacogenic (rather than eugenic) influence, combined with their promiscuity and fecundity, threatened to overwhelm and pollute the purer white racial stock. It was a classic example of moral panic: eugenicists whipped up widespread anxieties about sex, class, gender, and race to mobilize politicians and civic leaders.

By 1921, American eugenicists had so firmly implanted fears of racial pollution that 15 states had passed laws permitting involuntary sterilization. Between 1907 and 1927, over 8,000 such operations were performed. Many were carried out on "feebleminded" men and women—those we would today regard as severely developmentally disabled. But an untold number were carried out on men and women whose only apparent fault was belonging to the class popularly labeled white trash.

Such was the charge leveled in the most infamous court trial involving eugenics-based involuntary sterilization in the United States, the 1927 Supreme Court case *Buck v. Bell*. In the case, Buck protested her involuntary 1924 commitment to the Virginia Colony for Epileptics and Feeble-Minded. She had given birth out of wedlock and been sent away. The director of the colony, judging both Buck and her newborn feebleminded, and believing that Buck was herself the daughter of a feebleminded woman, wished to sterilize her immediately. Buck's presumed sexual promiscuity, the director argued, might lead to a line of children who would become burdens of the state. H. H. Laughlin, the nation's leading advocate for eugenical legislation, took up the case and, without ever meeting Buck, testified that, in his expert opinion, she was "part of the shiftless, ignorant, and worthless class of anti-social whites of the South." In May 1927, the Supreme Court ruled in favor of the eugenicists. Buck was soon sterilized. The shameful decision opened the door to forced sterilization across the nation. An estimated 60,000 Americans, most of them poor and indigent women, have since been sterilized without their consent and, in some cases, without their knowledge.

recycling the past?

We now know more of the facts in this historic case: Buck and her daughter were probably not feebleminded, even by the standard measures of her day. She had become pregnant not because of any sexual immorality but because her adoptive father had raped her. Her institutionalization was a way to hide his crime. Most involuntary sterilizations ended in the mid-1950s, although they continued into the 1980s. In 2002, 75 years after the Supreme Court's decision, the state of Virginia offered a formal apology to Buck's family and to all other families whose relatives had been forcibly sterilized. Since then, four other states have followed suit, with signs that North Carolina will be the next. California—where the largest number of eugenical sterilizations (over 20,000) occurred—formally apologized in 2003. While many states repealed or overturned involuntary sterilization laws, other states still fail to acknowledge this troubled past.

Sociologists such as Troy Duster have cautioned that the rise of genetic science in recent decades has opened a "backdoor" to eugenical thought, ushering in a new era of biological explanations for racial inequality. The dangers he warns of are real, but eugenics was never just about race or ethnic differences: it focused, first, on differences *within* whiteness. Eugenicists sought to establish some whites as superior elites and to assign others to the trash heap of history. Such efforts continue today: Charles Murray's recent bestseller *Coming Apart: The State of White America, 1960–2010* is a case in point. He shamelessly recycles stigmatypes—ones he first wrote about and stirred controversy with in a 1986 article titled "White Welfare, White Families, 'White Trash.'"

The long and disturbing history behind the term *white trash* rings with meaning today. We still see stigmatizing images of oversexed trailer trash, hear tasteless jokes about incest, and find a widely shared belief that all poor whites are dumber than "the rest of us." The stigma of white trash remains an active part of our fevered cultural imagination, even as some try to reclaim the phrase as a badge of rebellious honor. But few who use the term today—either proudly or as a shaming slur—seem to know about its deep historical entanglements with the politics of sex, race, and class.

RECOMMENDED READING

Troy Duster. 1990. *Backdoor to Eugenics*, New York: Routledge. Can today's genetic sciences avoid the errors and pitfalls of eugenics past? Duster asks the tough questions.

Edward J. Larson. 1995. *Sex, Race, and Science: Eugenics in the Deep South*, Baltimore: Johns Hopkins University Press. A Pulitzer Prize-winning historian tells the tale of how eugenics was implemented—and resisted—in the American South.

John Hartigan, Jr. 2005. *Odd Tribes: Towards a Cultural Analysis of White People*, Durham, NC: Duke University Press. Hartigan is the most astute observer of white people writing today, and these essays on "white trash" are must reads for any student of whiteness.

Nicole Hahn Rafter. 1988. *White Trash: The Eugenic Family Studies, 1877–1919*, Boston: Northeastern University Press. A finely edited anthology that brings together a large sampling of the original eugenic field studies (many unintentionally hilarious).

Philip Reilly. 1991. *The Surgical Solution: A History of Involuntary Sterilization in the United States*, Baltimore: Johns Hopkins University Press. Documents the scope and breadth of compulsory sterilization in the United States.

Matt Wray and Annalee Newitz (editors). 1997. *White Trash: Race and Class in America*, New York: Routledge. A collection of 13 essays about being poor and white in America. Includes personal memoirs, literary reflections, historical narratives, and observations from social scientists.

the fascination and frustration with native american mascots

JENNIFER GUILIANO

n the spring of 2013, a racial controversy emerged in that usually rarified realm of sport. It had to do with the "Redskins" moniker used by the NFL's Washington, D.C., franchise, one of the most prominent and profitable in the league. Long a symbol of frustration for Native American activists and advocates, the mascot inspired a powerful movement aimed at eliminating the offensive name. One D.C. city councilman urged the team to change their name to the "Redtails" and 10 members of Congress sent a letter to owner Daniel Snyder adding their voices to the plea. Snyder did not waver. Instead, he told the media his team would "NEVER" (his emphasis) change its name.

As with most U.S. controversies, everyone from celebrities to armchair quarterbacks has an opinion about the capitol city's team. Robert Griffin III, Washington's star quarterback, offered his opinion (via 140 characters on Twitter): "In a land of freedom we are held hostage by the tyranny of political correctness." Jonny Levin and the satirical staff at Funny or Die offered their take, calling for the Redskins' owner to make the team's name even *more* derogatory. Even right-wing rock legend Ted Nugent chimed in, telling one journalist that the call to do away with Native American mascots was being pushed by the "terminally disconnected" who "waste [their] time and energy focusing on things that matter about as much as a giant ball of string."

If you live in Michigan or Oregon, Wisconsin or Illinois, it is likely that within the last decade you've heard similar discussions and debates—often quite heated—about the use of Native American names, symbols, and performances for sports teams. You might even know a child whose school mascot is an Indian, Warrior, or Chief.

Be they elementary or professional teams, sporting clubs' use of Native American names, imagery, and metaphors as a vehicle for identification is pervasive. At the core of the discussion over the use of these representations are very serious racial divides. The historical conditions that influenced the creation and use of "Redskins" and other Indian monikers, in sport or otherwise, explicitly complicate the entire idea of the United States as the land of opportunity. The names, images, sounds, and metaphors gloss over the past, and their supporters care little about the impact of stereotypical imagery on members of the community that is being represented.

What is at stake in all of this is nothing less than an understanding of the history of Native Americans, the problems with racial stereotypes and caricatures, and the role of sport in the construction and contestation of race itself.

how mascots became racialized

The term *mascot*, derived from the French *mascotte* and Portuguese *masco*, originally referred to any object or talisman that brought luck to a person or household. The mascot was often an object of sorcery and mystery with otherworldly origins. Mascots were also religious talismans that wives and mothers bestowed upon men to protect them from death and disease in battle. "Mascot" over time came to mean young boys who followed troop divisions in wars, helping protect soldiers as human talismans.

When it came to sport, the young boys who would take on small team responsibilities—caring for bats and getting the team refreshments—in early games of baseball and football were equated with the battlefield helpers. These mascots brought good luck to their team as their predecessors had to their army.

Soon, though, sporting mascotry was racialized and relied on notions of racial hierarchy and identity that equated blackness to animalism. In one prime example, at the turn of the nineteenth century, the Chicago White Sox employed a former vaudeville performer, Clarence Duvall, as their mascot. "His grin is broad, his legs limbre and his face as black as the ace of spades," wrote one Chicago newsman. "Whenever anything goes wrong, it is only necessary to rub Clarence's wooly head to save the situation, and one of his celebrated 'double shuffles' to dispel all traces of care, even on the gloomiest occasion." Historian Adrian Burgos writes of a White Sox stop in Cairo, Egypt, where "several ballplayers forced [Duval] to wear a catcher's mask and glove and then paraded [him] about the Cairo railway station, tethered by a rope, 'as if he was some strange animal let loose from a menagerie.'" Mascots were treated as property to be mocked or even physically abused.

At the same time as white and African American mascots performed along the sidelines, Native athletes playing in professional sport in the late nineteenth and early twentieth century experienced racial degradation on the field. Louis Sockalexis, Charles A. Bender, John Tories Meyers, Jim Thorpe, and others faced racist taunts. Some were physically assaulted. All were treated as less than their white counterparts in everything from playing time to contract negotiations to housing. For those who saw the recent biopic *42*, such scenes might be vividly at hand, but they must be amplified. Native American players were treated as something between offensive and exotic, but they were always a target.

The "redskin" moniker is just one example of this. Although originally used as a physical descriptor by Europeans who encountered Native peoples, the term *redskins* has seen complex uses. Its first public recorded use was at the White House in 1812, but it also appeared in the work of James Fenimore Cooper, in records of treaty debates, in poetry, film, advertisements, and (as explored here) in the names and trademarks of sports teams.

Yet the benign use of "redskin" when President James Madison welcomed a delegation of tribes to discuss military alliances was marred by the behaviors of citizens who advertised bounties for redskins and hung Indian scalps as trophies in their homes and stores. While direct physical conflict declined after 1840 (particularly in the East post-Indian removal), the use of cultural tropes surrounding Indian identity grew. Natives were alternately portrayed as violent savages who should be quarantined on reservations far away from polite (read: white) society or as majestic, honorable, peaceable people who must be saved. Both tropes were enshrined in popular fiction, in visual performances like Wild West shows and films, in music, and in commercial

advertising. Indians whooped and hollered, hunted inno-
cents, communed with nature, and otherwise traversed the
pages of public imagination.

Today, when we talk about whether Native mascots are
appropriate, their history is glossed over. We'd like to think
the behaviors and experiences are past, that the United States
is a melting pot in which explicitly racialized exchanges have
given way to appreciation of great play and extraordinary
people. We like to think the country has either outgrown its
dark history or we conveniently forget about that history
altogether.

an oppressive past

"In 1492, Columbus sailed the ocean blue," begins the school
rhyme familiar to many. It goes on to say that Columbus
encountered the Arawaks in the Bahamas, where they all
enjoyed a peaceful exchange and Columbus departed. The
door was now open to centuries of European exploration
in the Americas. In this telling, it is a great story, but for
the Americas' indigenous peoples, European exploration—
motivated by quests for land, riches, and even religious
freedom—also introduced centuries of violence, oppression,
and conquest to their lives. Native Americans experienced
dramatic population declines, intra- and extra-tribal war-

fare, and exploitation at the hands of Spanish, French, and English colonists.

For all these traumatic factors, the story of Native peoples is also one of persistence and flourishing within the confines of colonialism. Empires have fallen and nations have been founded in the 500-plus years since that famous encounter. Native American societies live on.

According to the 2010 U.S. Census, 5.2 million people self-identify as Native American or Alaska Native (alone or in combination with other racial categorization). Nearly 2 million are members of 562 federally recognized tribes, and hold all of the rights of U.S. citizens, as well as those of their tribal citizenship. Indian tribes and individuals lay claim to over 56 million acres of land held in federal trust, and there are 326 tribal reservations administered by the U.S. government.

Unsettlingly, Native Americans also experience the highest rates of unemployment and poverty in the United States. Whether living on a reservation or in a city, their rates of alcoholism, diabetes, infant mortality, and adult mortality are dramatically higher than the rest of the U.S. population. In just the past few years, the government has moved to recognize, but not right, the wrongs perpetrated against these tribal citizens and their lasting effects. In the Defense Appropriations Act of 2010 (HR3326), the U.S. Senate formally acknowledged and apologized for its past treatment of

Native Americans (see p. 112 for the full text of the relevant section). Tellingly, though, HR3326 specifically pointed out that an apology would not be followed by any formal action. It closes: "Nothing in this section authorizes or supports any claim against the United States or serves as a settlement of any claim against the United States." We're sorry, it seems to say, but not *that* sorry.

For many indigenous peoples, the legacies of colonialism are alive and well. Their cultures are lumped together, at once totemic and disregarded. Comprising politically and culturally distinct groups, they are universally "Indian" in cultural memory—few others in the United States could describe the differences between the Menominee and Seminole tribes or explain whether a Mohawk is a group or a haircut. It is *that* history that is at play when we discuss whether Redskins and Warriors are appropriate team names, appropriate mascots. It is this legacy that makes so many cringe at a crowd of sports fans showing off the famous "Tomahawk Chop."

contemporary consequences

The injuries of colonization, the loss of life, misappropriation, and misinterpretation, though, are not just historical facts—they have contemporary consequences. The "Tomahawk Chop" mimics the scalping of battle opponents, a cultural memory of the violence of colonization for Indians and colonists alike. Sacred iconography, in the form of clothing and headdresses, are divorced from their communities of practice, their meanings distorted and corrupted. And, so very basically, the use of "redskins" is a racial slur. While sociologists and psychologists have noted that the use of Native mascots negatively impacts senses of self-worth, particularly among young children, more broadly, states like Michigan and Wisconsin have found that the use of Native mascots constitutes a harmful educational environment by presenting limited, racialized views of Natives.

The consequences of totalizing imagery, in which "one Indian is the same as another," have been readily documented by sociologists like Stephanie Fryberg, John Gonzalez, and Angela LaRoque. In case studies, Fryberg reveals that, regardless of the conditions of their creations and use (that is, whether it's the Haskell University mascot, which was created by Indians, or another mascot created and used by a predominantly white university), representations of Indian mascots lead Native participants to express depressed self-esteem, among other psychological costs. At the University of North Dakota, where athletic teams were called the "Fighting Sioux" until 2012, Gonzalez showed that Native students were "more likely targets of racial prejudice and potential discrimination," and LaRoque found that daily exposure to the "Fighting Sioux" logo led Native students to have higher levels of negative affect and psychological distress. Why, you might ask, aren't the schools happy to simply change their team name to something more benign, like Minnesota's "Golden Gophers" or Houston's "Oilers"?

Much of this comes together in the court cases that have begun to reshape the mascot landscape in recent decades.

from the court to the courts

In 1992, Suzan Shown Harjo, poet, activist, and former executive director of the National Congress of American Indians, joined Vine Deloria Jr. and others to sue Pro Football, Inc. to cancel the trademarks related to the term *redskins* and its portrayal. The petitioners claimed that the trademarks were disparaging to Native Americans under the Lanham Act, which states that a petition to register a trademark be refused if it "consists of or comprises immoral, deceptive, or scandalous matter; or matter which may disparage or falsely suggest a connection with persons, living or dead, institutions, beliefs, or national symbols, or bring them into contempt, or disrepute." After years of legal wrangling, the Trademark and Trial Board declared that the petition had not been lodged speedily enough before the courts—the term had been in use for decades, but only now brought before a court. The case was returned to the lower court to be revisited.

Fourteen years later, in 2006, six (now five—one later dropped out) new plaintiffs filed a new petition to cancel the trademark, backed by the legal evidence gathered in the Harjo case. *Blackhorse et al. v. Pro-Football, Inc.* alleges that, because each plaintiff had just reached the age of majority in 2006, there had been no unreasonable delay in their complaint. Thus, the petition claims that the case must rest on the evidence of the Redskins name and associated marks being disparaging, scandalous, and otherwise offensive to Natives. Oral arguments were heard March 7, 2013. By early to mid-2014, the Trademark and Trial Board will release its new conclusions. Undoubtedly, there will be additional appeals and counterappeals, no matter how the decision is reached. For our purposes, though, it is useful to consider two avenues of exploration: what constitutes injury and how it is proven, and where sport fits into the debate.

In the legal cases of Harjo and Blackhorse, the evidence of injury to the plaintiffs includes personal testimonies, the results of psychological surveys and polls, historical documents outlining the history of the term *redskins*, and other documents allegedly proving these trademarks are deleterious to Native peoples. And even as proof of injury was amassed, the plaintiffs can show, Indian mascotry spread in the twentieth century. From Dartmouth to Stanford, Indian mascots took the field. Over 70% of these institutions have now "retired" or removed their mascots, but that still leaves an awful lot of "Indians," "Warriors," and "Redskins."

arena of debate

Sport serves as a microcosm of contemporary life. It focuses issues of capitalism, market economies, cultural belonging, and play around consumptive behavior. It is simultaneously play and moral training . . . except when it is a billion-dollar-a-year business that relies on quantities of young, healthy bodies performing for the benefit of institutions and organizations. Sport generates massive streams of revenue wrapped in the rhetoric of enjoyment and character building. It is a privileged space with millions of contributors, from community-based Pee-Wee Leagues to ESPN's *First Look.*

So, when Dan Snyder says his team will *always* be the "Redskins," his assertions are not just about a perception that a small handful of "politically correct" activists are trying to force their way upon the rest of us. They are about a legacy of violence, oppression, and cultural heritage intertwined with the right of corporations to use that heritage for profit in a global economy. In a way, Snyder's defensive, blustering opinion makes sense—he's a businessman with a lot at stake. But why would fans get in on the action? Aren't the players the same, the games as competitive, the regional and city affiliations as strong, whether the mascot is a "Redskin" or a "Wizard"?

Defenses of Native American mascotry often rely on personal anecdotes and polling data (the "four out of every five respondents" who told the Associated Press they don't find mascotry offensive). They talk of "honoring Indians" and often trot out personal testimony from "an Indian friend" who says he or she doesn't find the various terms and images offensive. And they remind others that the teams themselves have a proud history as the "Redskins" or the like; the team's performances have redeemed the name, making it a testament to the prowess of Native Americans, not a slur implying savagery on the field.

When Snyder and others mythologize the Redskins name, they draw upon a massaged version of history in which the team's one-time owner George Preston Marshall, a virulent segregationist and neo-Confederate, meant to *honor* Natives and preserve their history. As sportswriter and columnist Dave Zirin has remarked, "the name represents the team's history of great players," yet fails to recognize how many of those players are offended by the banner under which they play.

Sociologists Ellen Staurowsky, Pauline Turner Strong, and Charles Fruehling Springwood have explored the motivations behind both whites and Natives supporting pro-mascot factions. In her look at the NCAA policy banning the use of Native American imagery and mascotry at post-season events, Staurowsky writes simply that the "cultural appropriation of American Indians is not neutral." The ability of whites to deploy Indianness relies on "primers of White privilege, where taking without asking or regard is not socially impolite, morally corrupt, educationally harmful, or legally criminal but an acceptable mode of behavior for masses of Americans." The notion that, as Americans, "we are all Indians" relies on disingenuous claims. Using Indians as mascot symbols amounts to social control. Non-Indians are denying the rights of Indians to express their own identity in a space free from judgment and commercialism.

Expanding on this, Turner Strong says appropriation is a clear indicator by dominant, white society that Native Americans cannot be fully recognized as valued citizen-participants in the United States. When pro-mascot advocates cry "political correctness run amok," they are also maintaining the political and economic inequalities that have denied Natives the right of self-determination for *centuries*.

An undercurrent of the entire argument is the ability to strategically claim Indian identity. Charles Fruehling

Springwood demonstrates that white people have fabricated Indian heritage (biological or metaphorical) tactically. Calling them "Indian wannabes," Springwood says these individuals claim Nativeness (usually via some long-lost relative or fabled ancestor) not to participate in Native community, but as an "opportunistic annunciation" that allows them to back pro-mascot movements and mute actual Indian voices. It's a strange mutation of the "Some of my best friends are black" segues used in blustering defenses of anti-black sentiment today. And these revisionist *personal* histories are often intertwined with revisionist *corporate* histories.

Revisionist histories are not unique to the Redskins. They are a universal construct within the pro-mascot debate. Histories of universities, colleges, even local public schools, have been rewritten. The public is led to believe that these historical origin tales are all sunshine and light, rather than continuing skirmishes in a centuries-old battle for Native peoples to not just live, but to represent themselves freely and openly.

Since the earliest accounts of explorers' encounters with Native Americans, there's been an almost patronizing fascination. Today it's not just in memoirs and diaries, but on television, in films, in commercials, and at halftime. It plays out in ticket sales and Sunday afternoon commentary. It plays out in courts and on campuses. And it will play out until

Native Americans gain the right to define themselves and their lives within mainstream cultural production.

RECOMMENDED READING

Stephanie A. Fryberg, Hazel Rose Markus, Daphna Oyserman, and Joseph M. Stone. 2008. "Of Warrior Chiefs and Indian Princesses: The Psychological Consequences of American Indian Mascots," *Basic and Applied Social Psychology* 30(3):208–218. Four case studies that explore the consequences of American Indian mascots on Native high school and college students, as well as community members.

C. Richard King and Charles Fruehling Springwood (editors). 2001. *Team Spirits: The Native American Mascots Controversy*, Lincoln, NE: University of Nebraska Press. Highlights case studies of the Washington Redskins, the Cleveland Indians, and the University of Illinois's Chief Illiniwek, as well as the Florida State Seminoles and Marquette University.

Charles Fruehling Springwood. 2004. "'I'm Indian Too!': Claiming Native American Identity, Crafting Authority in Mascot Debates," *Journal of Sport and Social Issues* 28(1):56–70. Examines the ways in which Americans, particularly white Americans, have strategically claimed Indianness to argue in favor of Native American mascots, thereby disenfranchising Natives from their own identity.

Ellen J. Staurowsky. 2007. "'You Know, We Are All Indian': Exploring White Power and Privilege in Reactions to the NCAA Native American Mascot Policy," *Journal of Sport and Social Issues* 31(1):61–76. Explores the effects of the 2005 National Collegiate Athletic Association's post-season ban on Indian mascots by highlighting what responses to the ban reveal about white people, power, and privilege.

Pauline Turner Strong. 2004. "The Mascot Slot: Cultural Citizenship, Political Correctness, and Pseudo-Indian Sports Symbols," *Journal of Sport and Social Issues* 28(1):79–87. Drawing on Aihwa Ong's concept of cultural citizenship and Michael-Rolph Trouillot's notion of the "savage slot," Strong argues that mascotry serves as a form of cultural citizenship and control that offers obstacles to full participatory citizenship by Native Americans.

section 8113 of the defense appropriations act of 2010 (hr3326):

Apology to Native Peoples of the United States

Sec. 8113. (a) Acknowledgment and Apology— The United States, acting through Congress—

(1) recognizes the special legal and political relationship Indian tribes have with the United States and the solemn covenant with the land we share;

(2) commends and honors Native Peoples for the thousands of years that they have stewarded and protected this land;

(3) recognizes that there have been years of official depredations, ill-conceived policies, and the breaking of covenants by the Federal Government regarding Indian tribes;

(4) apologizes on behalf of the people of the United States to all Native Peoples for the many instances of vio-

lence, maltreatment, and neglect inflicted on Native Peoples by citizens of the United States;

(5) expresses its regret for the ramifications of former wrongs and its commitment to build on the positive relationships of the past and present to move toward a brighter future where all the people of this land live reconciled as brothers and sisters, and harmoniously steward and protect this land together;

(6) urges the President to acknowledge the wrongs of the United States against Indian tribes in the history of the United States in order to bring healing to this land; and

(7) commends the State governments that have begun reconciliation efforts with recognized Indian tribes located in their boundaries and encourages all State governments similarly to work toward reconciling relationships with Indian tribes within their boundaries.

(b) Disclaimer—Nothing in this section—

(1) authorizes or supports any claim against the United States; or

(2) serves as a settlement of any claim against the United States.

environmental inequalities

HOLLIE NYSETH BREHM AND DAVID N. PELLOW

8

Think back to the movie *Erin Brockovich*. The basic plot, based on a true story, goes like this: A woman with no legal training learns that many residents in a small town have gotten cancer due to exposure to contaminated groundwater. After investigating a large factory believed to be responsible for the contamination, Brockovich proceeds to kick ass. She files a lawsuit against the company, bringing justice to the sick families.

It's the perfect drama-filled Hollywood plot. Yet what is even more dramatic is that the basic story of communities living in contamination isn't rare at all. In many places around the world and in the U.S., people share their neighborhoods with hazardous waste, toxic incinerators, and health-threatening chemical contamination. Moreover, some people are much more likely to be affected by these environmental hazards than others—namely, people of color, working-class people, immigrants, and indigenous communities.

This uneven exposure to environmental risks and hazards, often coupled with the systematic exclusion of people from environmental decision-making processes, is called environmental racism or environmental inequality. But don't be fooled by the terms—the causes of environmental inequality are social and political. In other words, environmental inequality is *not*, at its core, an environmental issue. Rather, it is rooted in our discourses, structures, and political and economic institutions, and it is intertwined with the other inequalities that permeate our daily lives.

the emergence of environmental (in)justice

Although *Erin Brockovich* hit the theaters in 2000, environmental inequalities are far from new and far from over. Native Americans, African Americans, Latinos, and European immigrants in the United States have long been disproportionately exposed to the harmful effects of living near city dumps, working in coal mines and on farms picking pesticide-drenched produce, and bearing the brunt of undemocratic and destructive land-use decisions. But it wasn't until researchers, activists, and government officials began documenting patterns of social inequality and environmental harm in the 1970s and early 1980s that the concept of environmental inequality emerged.

For example, the U.S. General Accounting Office conducted one of the earliest studies of environmental inequality in 1983. The study examined the racial composition of communities near four major hazardous waste landfills in the South. In three of the four cases, the communities around the landfills were predominantly African American (in the fourth, the community was disproportionately African American). Several other groundbreaking studies in the 1980s and 1990s confirmed these patterns at the local, regional, national, and even international scales.

In response, scholars and activists began calling for environmental justice. According to sociologist Robert Bullard, environmental justice is the notion that all people and communities are entitled to equal protection by environmental health laws and regulations. Many researchers and advocates have rallied around this concept, which has influenced a body of scholarship on environmental inequalities as well as an ever-growing social movement to combat them.

initial documentation and response to environmental inequalities

Scholars and movement activists began to address environmental inequalities by first documenting their existence. Since the 1980s, there have been literally thousands of studies that have provided strong evidence of racial inequalities in exposure to environmental hazards. Many other scholars have argued that environmental inequalities do not just disproportionately affect racial minorities. Other social categories, like gender, age, class, immigration status/citizenship, and indigeneity, are also associated with disproportionate exposure to hazards. Taken together, these effects overlap and are difficult to disentangle. Here, we focus on race and class, as these are the most prominent in existing studies.

Rather than reviewing these studies (which could fill books), we turn to two examples in the city of Chicago. The southeast portion of Chicago is known locally as "the Toxic Doughnut" because it is surrounded on all sides by hundreds of polluting industrial facilities, including paint manufacturers, landfills, a sewage treatment plant, a steel manufacturing company, incinerators, and several dumps. Each year, these local industries emit hundreds of thousands of pounds of chemicals into the air. Local residents, who are predominantly African Americans living in public housing, report high incidences of asthma, chronic obstructive pulmonary disease, skin rashes, and cancer.

Scholars like Bullard, Beverly Wright, Bunyan Bryant, and Dorceta Taylor (among others) founded the field of environmental justice studies in order to document inequalities like these. Yet, unlike the Hollywood portrayal, it is actually very

difficult to link health problems to specific chemical or industrial sites, especially when several exist in the same area.
While this means that the resolution depicted in *Erin Bro-
kovich* is not representative, it also means that there are
many other responses to environmental inequalities.

In the mid-1980s in the Toxic Doughnut, for example, several activists engaged in an act of civil disobedience against
a chemical waste incinerator operator. They coordinated a
"lockdown" and chained themselves to vehicles placed in the
path of trucks transporting hazardous materials for incin-
eration. By the end of the day, the coalition had turned away
no less than 57 waste trucks.

Such acts of civil disobedience have been common
responses to perceived environmental injustices, though this
particular story doesn't end at the incinerator gates. The
activists involved in the lockdown joined a broader network of
organizations that comprise the environmental justice movement, and they collectively pushed then-president Bill Clinton
to sign an executive order (12898) directing federal agencies
to develop and implement plans to guard against the production of environmental inequalities. It was a historic accomplishment for the environmental justice movement, though
the fight for environmental justice was (and is) far from over.

In fact, 20 years later in the same city, things hadn't
changed much. Many of Chicago's Latino communities are

concentrated in the neighborhoods of Pilsen and Little Village on the West Side of Chicago. In the early 2000s, activists in these communities began a campaign to shut down two coal-fired power plants. Pollution from the Fisk (in Pilsen) and Crawford (in Little Village) plants are, according to researchers from Chicago's Clean Air Task Force, largely responsible for 42 premature deaths, 66 heart attacks, and 720 asthma attacks *each year*. Community organizations from environmental, faith, health, and labor movements across the city came together to form the Clean Power Coalition (CPC) not only to phase out the power plants, but also to make Chicago a coal-free city. The CPC eventually received support from 35 aldermen and the mayor. In 2012, the organization achieved its goal. An agreement was signed to close the Fisk plant within the year and the Crawford plant in 2014. It was a major victory for the environmental justice movement and for one of the lead organizations in the CPC, the Little Village Environmental Justice Organization.

causes of environmental inequalities

As the fight for environmental justice rages on, scholars have turned their attention to better understanding why environmental inequalities exist. Various explanations have been proposed, and here we focus on two—economic- and discrimination-based explanations. Socio-political explanations are also at play, but since power and politics are everywhere, we integrate them into the first two. As noted above, none of these are fundamentally environmental causes—they are rooted in society.

ECONOMIC-BASED EXPLANATIONS

A common explanation for environmental inequality is that hazardous corporations do not intentionally discriminate. Instead, they place facilities where land is cheap and where labor pools are available. Both help companies in their quest to maximize profits. Often, marginalized communities already live in such areas, and once a hazardous facility is present, they likely lack the resources to move.

Focusing on the broader system, sociologists Allan Schnaiberg and Kenneth Gould developed a related economic-based explanation called the treadmill of production thesis. Under this model, there is an ever-growing need for capital investment to generate goods for sale in the marketplace, and that requires continuous inputs of energy and expansion. This expansion of the economy drives two fundamental dynamics: the creation of economic wealth and the creation of the negative byproducts of the production process. The social and economic benefits are unevenly distributed in favor of businesses and affluent communities, while the environmental risks and other negative byproducts are disproportionately concentrated among the groups of people with the least ability to resist the location of polluting facilities in their community. Thus, polluting facilities are sited among the most vulnerable groups: the poor, unskilled laborers, and the skilled blue-collar residents.

Scholar and theorist Ulrich Beck further expands this idea with a model of the interactions among technology, social dynamics, and ecological degradation. For Beck, a key aspect of the process of modernization is the application of scientific research and knowledge to expand economic growth. Driven by the need to maximize profits, corporations continually develop new technologies that produce unforeseen risks for the entire society. This breaks down society's ability to ensure the safety of its citizens from the production of industrial hazards and creates a "risk society" in which the politics of the distribution of economic production is overlaid by a politics regarding the distribution of environmental pollution. Thus, environmental injustice.

DISCRIMINATION-BASED EXPLANATIONS

Other researchers focus more directly on racism and institutional discrimination as drivers of environmental inequality. As evidence, they point to the persistent and stark racial divides in environmental policy making. For example, scholars like Charles Mills and Robert Higgins point to the ways that racism informs environmental decision making on a deeper cultural register. Mills draws on philosophy and historical texts to connect racism to a psychological, cultural, and legal framework linking images of people of color (specifically people of African descent) with barbarism, filth, dirt, and pollution. According to Mills, many white people view African peoples as a form of pollution, making it morally easier to contain industrial waste and factory pollution in their segregated, already "polluted" neighborhoods. This link between non-European peoples and symbols associated with nature, such as danger, disease, and the primitive savage, is common throughout European history and literature, as well as within contemporary politics in the global North, whether one is speaking of Africans, African Americans, indigenous peoples, Asians, Latin Americans, or the Roma of Europe.

Like Mills, environmental philosopher Robert Higgins argues that minority environments are seen as "appropriately polluted" spaces. Immigrants, indigenous populations, and peoples of color are viewed by many policy makers, politicians, and ecologists as a *source* of environmental contamination. That view influences decisions to place noxious facilities and toxic waste in the spaces these populations occupy or relegate these groups to spaces where environmental quality is low and undesirable.

Racial disparities are also mirrored in myriad other aspects of environmental justice-relevant U.S. institutions, including education, health care, and criminal justice. Often, however, particular acts of racism and discrimination cannot easily be located and measured, as racism is not a specific *thing* and its effects cannot be neatly isolated or extracted from social life. In addition, people in poverty can be discriminated against, though in scholarship to date, discrimination-based explanations have focused on race, not poverty.

As we consider economic- and discrimination-based explanations for environmental injustice, politics are clearly at play in both. The political power of communities, states, and industries is inseparable from racial and economic forces driving environmental inequalities. For one, industries and corporations might purposefully seek the path of least resistance. As affluent communities, often white, have the resources and social capital to oppose the placement of hazardous facilities in or near their neighborhoods, companies place hazards in locations where they believe they will meet little or no local political resistance. Communities that are already socially marginalized are often excluded from participation in policy making, zoning, and urban planning, while industries, corporations, and similar entities are highly involved in these processes. It's just *easier* to site industrial operations in neighborhoods where the residents have long held little political clout. In addition, working-class communities and communities of color are relatively invisible in mainstream environmental movements. If the voices of disadvantaged communities are not heard or respected in political *or* protest circles, they can be overlooked. Multiple forms of hierarchy and politics drive environmental inequalities.

expanding environmental justice

Though the scholarly field (and related social movements) of environmental justice began by focusing on unequal exposure to environmental hazards, some scholars and activists have expanded its boundaries. In 1993, sociologist Stella Čapek introduced the environmental justice frame, which she saw as a lens through which activists and scholars constructed meaning about environmental justice. According to Čapek, the environmental justice frame consists of six key claims:

- The right to accurate information from authorities concerning environmental risks
- Public hearings

- Democratic participation in decision making regarding the future of any threatened community
- Compensation for injured parties from those who inflict harm
- Expressions of solidarity with survivors of environmental injustices
- A call to abolish environmental injustice

Čapek's model highlights something that we have hinted at—environmental injustice is not just about disproportionate hazards; it is also about access to decision-making capabilities, democratic process, and power.

More recently, scholars have analyzed how other aspects of social life (beyond race and class) influence environmental inequalities. For example, environmental hazards can affect women differently than men. In places like Silicon Valley, where the electronics industry boom began decades ago, the majority of workers in the most chemically intensive jobs were immigrant women (some were exposed to upward of 700–1,000 different chemicals in a single workstation). Gender also plays a strong role in how people *confront* environmental hazards. As research by Phil Brown and Faith Ferguson and Celene Krauss demonstrates, women have been the most visible and vocal advocates for the environmental justice movement. This is largely because of their social structural position as likely caretakers of children and the elderly (often the first members of families and communities to show signs of environmental illness) and the most likely to have strong connections to community-based institutions like schools, churches, health clinics, and salons—sites where information and concerns about environmental threats are shared and where people are often mobilized.

Environmental justice scholars are working to expand the concept in other ways as well. Notably, while we have focused on the United States in this piece, scholars are increasingly seeing environmental inequalities as global issues. For example, the practice of hazardous waste dumping across national borders is a form of transnational environmental inequality. Every year, wealthy nations and corporations produce millions of tons of toxic waste from industry, consumers, municipalities, state institutions, computers and electronics products, and agricultural practices. These hazards directly and indirectly contribute to high rates of human and nonhuman morbidity and mortality and to ecosystem damage on every continent and in every ocean system. Dumping waste in other people's "backyards" is reflective of economically, racially, and politically unequal relations between and within global North and South communities.

Climate change is another example of global environmental inequality. While contributing the least to the causes of climate disruption, people of color, women, indigenous communities, and global South nations often feel the brunt of climate disruption. They bear the burdens of ecological, economic, and health effects, thereby giving rise to the concept of *climate injustice*. These communities are among the first to experience the effects of climate disruption, which can include "natural" disasters, rising levels of respiratory illness and infectious disease, heat-related morbidity and mortality, and large increases in energy costs. Flooding from severe storms, rising sea levels, and melting glaciers affects millions in Asia and Latin America, while sub-Saharan Africa is experiencing sustained droughts. Yet, nearly 75% the world's annual CO_2 emissions come from the global North, where only 15% of the earth's population resides.

The ability to adapt to climate change is also highly uneven across social groups within countries. For example, African Americans have fewer resources to cope with or recover from a host of negative health impacts that might result from climate change. For example, they are 50% more likely than non-African Americans to lack health insurance. The delivery of disaster relief is less available to African Americans, too. This was made evident in the aftermath of Hurricane Katrina, when the Federal Emergency Management Agency failed to provide services to thousands of African Americans in the Gulf region who were without shelter, food, or drinkable water for days. Research demonstrates that racial stereotypes continue to contribute to reduced disaster relief aid for African Americans in the wake of all manner of climate-related disasters.

Gender inequalities impact the ability to adapt to climate change as well. In Bangladesh, for instance, women's domestic duties have historically made them especially vulnerable to extreme weather events like storms and floods. Responsibilities as the primary child caregivers; primary gatherers of food, fuel, and water; and the primary cooks and tenders of livestock have typically tied women to low-lying residences, which are more vulnerable to the rising waters associated with extreme weather. The relative poverty of women in Bangladesh also makes them less resilient in the face of climate change, since they have poorer nutrition, limited health care, and, in the case of divorced and widowed women, fewer sources of social support.

a global response

Today, the real Erin Brockovich continues to participate in other environmental justice lawsuits, and activists living in the Toxic Doughnut and on Chicago's West Side are still orchestrating grassroots campaigns for environmental justice, including a push to improve the city's public transit system and promote sustainable energy production. The movement is much broader, with grassroots activists, scholars, governmental agencies, and even corporate actors converging around these pressing issues. At the global level, too, international treaties have come to recognize global environmental injustices tied to climate change and the transfer of hazardous waste to the global South. Yet, despite some of the successes of these transnational advocacy movements, environmental inequalities persist.

Multiple solutions at all levels are needed to comprise a global response to environmental inequality. The United States can and should do its part. While new laws may be needed over time, right now we believe we must start with the enforcement of *existing* laws that are relevant to environmental justice. The executive order referenced earlier was intended to ensure that federal agencies function in a way that protects communities against environmental inequalities. Unfortunately, as the U.S. government's own inspector general has concluded, federal agencies are doing a poor job of implementing Order 12898, and there have been varying and uneven levels of commitment from the White House, Congress, and the U.S. Environmental Protection Agency since it was signed in 1994.

The first of many needed responses to environmental injustice, then, is for the federal government to enforce a host of existing laws intended to protect the environment, human health, and vulnerable communities. Laws like the National Environmental Policy Act, the Clean Air Act, and the Fair Housing Act have been under attack by industry and special interest groups since their passage, and each has been weakened over the years. It has become more difficult—not less—for working-class people and people of color to find jobs, homes, and recreational spaces that are free from toxic hazards. Many other solutions—far more than we can review here—are needed, but enforcing the laws already on the books is a good start.

RECOMMENDED READING

Phil Brown and Faith I.T. Ferguson. 1995. "'Making a Big Stink': Women's Work, Women's Relationships, and Toxic Waste Activism," *Gender and Society* 9(2):145–72. An excellent analysis of the many ways that gender shapes the way we define and respond to environmental hazards.

Robert D. Bullard and Beverly Wright. 2012. *The Wrong Complexion for Protection: How the Government Response to Disaster Endangers African American Communities,* New York: New York University Press. A pioneering study of the history of institutional racism in disaster readiness, response, and recovery and its effects on African Americans.

Stella Čapek. 1993. "The 'Environmental Justice' Frame: A Conceptual Discussion and an Application," *Social Problems* 40(1):5–24. A theoretically rich and grounded study that captures a core of the environmental justice movement's interpretation of harm and its vision of what justice might look like.

Paul Mohai and Robin Saha. 2007. "Racial Inequality in the Distribution of Hazardous Waste: A National-Level Reassessment," *Social Problems* 54(3):343–370. A methodologically innovative study that applies new techniques for measuring community proximity to hazardous waste sites and finds that racial disparities (i.e., environmental racism) for these land uses are much worse than previously thought.

David N. Pellow. 2007. *Resisting Global Toxics: Transnational Movements for Environmental Justice*, Cambridge, MA: MIT Press. A detailed analysis that traces transnational waste dumping and the global environmental justice movements that have emerged in response.

J. Timmons Roberts and Bradley Parks. 2007. *A Climate of Injustice: Global Inequality, North-South Politics, and Climate Policy*, Cambridge, MA: MIT Press. A groundbreaking analysis of the intersections between climate change and social inequality and how this directly affects the process of climate negotiations.

thinking about trayvon: privileged responses and media discourse with charles a. gallagher, zenzele isoke, enid logan, and aldon morris

STEPHEN SUH

M uch has occurred in the months following the initial media frenzy surrounding Trayvon Martin's death.* George Zimmerman was eventually arrested for second-degree murder and is currently out on bond while awaiting trial. His wife has been charged with perjury for lying about their finances (and the over $200,000 sent to them for legal defense by sympathetic citizens) in a bail hearing. Discussions on "stand your ground" laws

*Editors' note: This article was originally published shortly after Martin's 2012 death. Zimmerman has since been acquitted.

abound. And there's even been a public backlash against Martin's presumed innocence in his death, with numerous reports claiming that he was a juvenile delinquent. Others felt his "hoodied" look had made Martin appear threatening, and thus perhaps deserving of being profiled.

The "hoodie," in particular, has become an important symbolic tool for those seeking justice for Trayvon Martin and his family, as well as others like him. Thousands of individuals, ranging from professional basketball players to white suburban youth, have sported hoodies in solidarity.

We called on a number of prominent social scientists to discuss the aftermath of Trayvon Martin's death, examining the multiple narratives that factored into early media coverage and public responses. We started by asking our panelists *why they thought Trayvon Martin's death elicited such a large public response, especially among white, middle-class Americans.*

Aldon Morris: The middle-class image of Trayvon Martin and the middle-class quality of the response by his parents are largely responsible for the extraordinary [public] response. The early images of Martin depicted him as a young, innocent, handsome, wholesome, gentle kid that all parents, friends, and relatives [would want to] embrace and protect.... Middle-class America [thought] "this kid looks and acts like my own son despite being a young black male."

Trayvon's mother and father also looked and acted like decent middle-class parents. They spoke good English, dressed in middle-class garb, and portrayed no threatening black militancy. Yet, though persistent and vociferous in their outrage, Trayvon's parents spoke softly and movingly, conveying a grief that tugged at the hearts of ordinary people. . . . The Martins pulled off a near miracle in white America. . . . They were able to subjugate their blackness to their humanity.

Charles Gallagher: Trayvon Martin's death has struck such dissimilar chords with black and white America because both groups see race relations, treatment by law enforcement, and the ability to attain the American dream in starkly different terms. For much of white America, this is a case of cognitive dissonance; [they believe] race-based discrimination and institutional racism are actions of the past. While the nearly 200 million non-Hispanic whites in the United States are an extremely diverse lot, national polling data on their attitudes and perceptions concerning race, race relations, and the relative socio-economic mobility of blacks point generally in one direction: that the . . . nation has transcended the caste-like trappings of race and is now best defined by "color-blind egalitarianism." This means most whites have come to view race as a benign social marker.... Most importantly in this "leveled playing field" perspective is that, just as blacks are no longer socially or economically disadvantaged in any systemic way . . . whites are no longer privileged by their whiteness.

[Still, though] there is no shortage of objective measures that demonstrate racism is still very much interwoven into the fabric of our social institutions. Who gets "stopped and frisked" or is targeted for predatory lending or must deal with the effects of environmental racism? It's disproportionately minorities. The cognitive dissonance . . . is reflected in the stark racial differences in recent polling data concerning the death and treatment of Trayvon Martin.

Zenzele Isoke: The media's fixation on "white middle America" is an example of one of the ways that the American media upholds white supremacy—a political and economic system that upholds the privileges of those who are white and/or enjoy white privilege. This needs to change. I think that too little of our discussion is centered upon the experiences and perspectives of people of color—especially poor and working-class people of color who are routine victims of racial profiling and other forms of government-endorsed racial terrorism. I believe that the media should be more concerned about how African Americans, Latinos, Pacific Islanders, and Native American people feel about Trayvon Martin's murder. More of the conversation should be based on why there has been such a poignant and heart-wrenching response in these communities, especially in various African American communities—wealthy and poor, urban, rural, and suburban. Why has there been such a huge response in our communities?

Enid Logan: Unlike many other parallel tragedies, I believe, this case elicited a large public response because it fit into a familiar and galvanizing narrative about what racism is and what a "good person" should do about it. In addition to there being a readily identifiable white racist in this narrative, there was also a pure, unblemished black victim in the person of Martin.

Participants went on to tell us they had wished for a more nuanced, critical media discussion about race, particularly in relation to violence committed against people of color.

Logan: This death should lead us to think more deeply about the racial implications of so-called "race-neutral"

[laws]—like the "stand your ground" ordinance—throughout the country. A manifestation of the institutionalized and covert nature of modern racism, our "color-blind" legal system often functions in ways that discipline, punish, exclude, incarcerate, or justify the murder of nonwhites in particular. Furthermore, so-called "black-on-black violence" has been wrongly declared out of bounds in this discussion (see, for example, Khalil Gibran Muhammad's April 5 editorial in the *New York Times*). As George Yancey and others have written, it is very hard to "see" black male bodies in any way other than as suspicious, threatening, out of control, and in need of containment and discipline. If we really care about the untimely deaths of so many black youth, then we cannot limit the conversation only to cases involving so-called "white racists."

Isoke: What has not been sufficiently covered is an overall mapping of the number of deaths committed by law enforcement officers, and in George Zimmerman's case, "wannabe" police officers who racially profile, target, and kill African American and Latino youth. For instance, why haven't the media and federal agencies compiled national statistics about the number of unarmed people of color—African Americans, Latinos, and Native Americans—who have been killed by the police? George Zimmerman, in my opinion, represented the sentiment held by many working-class white men, that young black people are a threat. This is why so many white people—specifically white men who work in law enforcement—spoke out in support of Zimmerman. And although I can't prove it (no one can), I'm certain that those are the people who donated to his defense fund. I would bet on it, and I'm not a gambling woman!

[So] why doesn't the media begin to think about these frequent killings—and in some cases, targeted assassinations—as forms of state-sponsored terrorism instead of so-called "justifiable homicide"? Also, I feel like the media doesn't give enough air time to organizations—social justice organizations—other than the NAACP, the Urban League, and the Congressional Black Caucus. There are organizations in cities and urban communities across America that take a lot of time to document and study racial profiling and other forms of police brutality that result in the maiming and killing of young black people. [These include] organizations like Communities United Against Police Brutality, the Malcolm X Grassroots Movement, the Audre Lorde Project, Occupy the Hood, and so many others.

Morris: The reality that what happened to young Trayvon Martin is commonplace in America and not an anomaly [wasn't] covered sufficiently. [It seemed as if his death was] a horrendous but isolated tragedy. During a town hall meeting in Sanford, Florida, shortly after Trayvon's murder, a distraught black mother cried out that her son had been murdered just a few months prior . . . but no outcry for justice took hold. It was the kind of story that should have made the . . . news. Yet there was no coverage at all and certainly not a discussion regarding whether Martin's death was a link in a long chain.

Many story lines were adopted by the media and the public in discussing the Trayvon Martin case. Initial reports focused on Trayvon Martin's apparent innocence (as both the victim and a minor), George Zimmerman's presumed guilt, and the shooter's contested whiteness.

Morris: The initial media coverage focused . . . [on a] compelling story line . . . that this promising, unarmed kid had been needlessly struck down by Zimmerman, a much older and armed white man. Details of Zimmerman's background, family life, and character trickled out slowly in comparison to Trayvon's, and even [months later] not a great deal of personal information is known about what kind of person Zimmerman is. This initial coverage helped foster a saint/devil scenario that is always good copy for the media; it helped trigger the enormous response.

But this story line is not static. The media [later began] to suggest that maybe we have a false image of Trayvon—[maybe] Trayvon should be viewed as a pot-smoking, poor-performing, rebellious student prone to violence . . . maybe Trayvon was more like violent young black "thugs" than what we were led to believe. Images of Zimmerman, on the other hand, are beginning to suggest that maybe he faced a young violent black monster . . . intent on killing him. Thus, Trayvon represents the nightmare that many white Americans wish to avoid at all costs. These competing story lines will become even more important as this case is adjudicated.

Logan: Trayvon's innocence was most powerfully established via the photographs that were circulated of him as a child and as a tween, wearing an earnest expression and/or a football uniform, [even] though he was 17 at the time of his murder. He was carrying in his pockets only Skittles and iced tea, we were told, he'd gone to the store for his little brother, he was an honor-roll student, and his family was non-poor (i.e., either upper-working or lower-middle class). Thus the murder fit into a civil rights–era narrative about white-on-black violence—a narrative about innocent black children being gunned down by white racists. Hence the parallels to Emmett Till and the four little girls killed in Birmingham.

I make this point not to imply that Trayvon was "less than innocent" and therefore in some way responsible for his own death. My argument, rather, is that Trayvon's extreme innocence was a precondition for the recognition of his humanity. The body of 17-year-old Trayvon was supplanted by that of him as a child, because at puberty his body had lost even the plausibility of innocence (Beverly Tatum discusses this in her 2003 book *Why Are All the Black Kids Sitting Together in the Cafeteria?*). The child Trayvon could be granted provisional whiteness: the presumption that he had a right to be in white space, that he may not have been up to no good, that he could have just been a boy walking home in the dark. By championing a black victim who had been wronged by racism, the liberal press could (as it had during Barack Obama's presidential campaign) celebrate its "thoroughly confirmed" commitment to racial tolerance and justice.

But the almost romanticized notion of an ideal white racist/black victim began to fall apart as the starkly dichotomous framing of the case was complicated and as Trayvon [came to be] viewed as less than saintly. Consider the impact of the finding that he had been suspended from school at the time of his murder. As Trayvon's father stated, the question should not be why was he on suspension, but why was he killed!

Isoke: These "story lines" are techniques the media uses to garner attention; [they] are contrived and help absolve the media of its own responsibility in presenting the truth, as well as the real-life social consequences of its coverage.

The truth is that, yet again, an unarmed black man was killed by a white man for no other reason than the young black male was considered a threat. Zimmerman carried a live firearm to protect himself from those he feared. He acted on his fear in the most horrific way and shot Travyon dead. That is tragic. The political community, including the media, should recognize this simple injustice. When the media panders to both sides or both "story lines" . . . it makes a mockery of the political community. The media operates on the fiction that both sides are "equally valid," when clearly they are not.

What about the "hoodie movement" and the eventual co-optation of the "hoodie" as an emblem of racial oppression and human agency?

Isoke: Every symbol of resistance and freedom struggle gets co-opted. That is no surprise. It can even be a good thing.

I even wore a black hoodie in support of Trayvon, and I never wear hoodies! I was glad to see people of many races and economic backgrounds wearing the hoodie. I felt as if there was a part of people who recognized the injustice and the reality of race-based oppression in the United States. I saw Christians, Muslims, granola folks . . . everybody wearing the hoodie. It felt good. I hope that everyone who sported the hoodie . . . will take that sentiment and challenge racial profiling by citizens and law enforcement alike—then translate that into sound public policy. I hope that citizens begin to call for the prosecution of police officers who abuse and kill innocent civilians . . . of prosecutors who railroad poor black and brown people into prison.

Logan: I would argue, rather than being an expression of color blindness among whites, the "hoodie movement" was all about race. The "hoodie" today is a clearly identifiable trope of hip hop culture and urban black masculinity. Charles Gallagher writes about white youth . . . believing that through the consumption of racialized cultural artifacts (music, clothing, foods, etc.), they may experience what it is to be a person of color. Race is understood by whites as pertaining to culture, rather than mapping onto a privilege and power hierarchy from which they directly benefit. [So] the appropriation of the hoodie and claim to "be" Trayvon Martin was both an appropriation of black racial authenticity and an aspect of the consumption of blackness in the twenty-first century. Recall that most everyone standing in their hoodie was looking "mean" or "serious"—like the prototypical, pissed-off urban black male. Why was no one smiling? Why not emphasize the youthfulness of Trayvon? While white youth in the 1960s traveled to the Deep South to participate in the Freedom Rides and put their very lives at risk, there are no such costs associated with [today's periodic] forms of anti-racist activism (i.e., "I am Trayvon Martin" and "Yes We Can!").

To conclude, panelists reflected on what the events following Trayvon Martin's death said about the current state of American race relations.

Gallagher: According to Gallup, a majority of white Americans (51%) believe that race did not play or played only a minor role in the initial confrontation or shooting of Trayvon Martin. By the second week of coverage . . . a near-majority of whites (43%) said there was too much coverage of Martin's death. Perhaps these white responses reflect racial fatigue or the news overexposure of a topic given our 24/7 media cycle. It may, however, reflect the anxiety, misdirected anger, or even shock that in the age of perceived color-blind egalitarianism, a young black man minding his own business in his dad's development, "armed" with a can of iced tea and Skittles, could be forced into a deadly encounter because of his skin color.

Isoke: I think there is a critical mass of people—possibly even a majority—who understand that racism and racial violence (especially state-sponsored racial violence) is an ugly smear on this country's history and its reputation today. I think that the "activist" response was predictable, but I think that the widespread community response was a bit different.... There are so many Americans who are sick of the senseless killing of African Americans, especially African American men. America is more diverse and racially progressive than we are led to believe in the media—this is another symptom of white supremacy. I think that many Americans, regardless of race, are outraged at Zimmerman's behavior, as well as the behavior of the Sanford Police Department and the so-called "stand your ground" law. Many Americans are appalled and outraged that citizens are permitted to walk around with loaded pistols waiting for something bad to happen so they can pull out their weapon and shoot someone.

However, the media doesn't cover this enough. It's like the side that stands for peace, tolerance, and non-violence doesn't get heard over those who advocate policy positions and attitudes based upon fear, intolerance, and ignorance about people who are poorer, less privileged, and less racist. Those who talk the loudest who invoke the most fear, and who have the most money, get heard. This needs to change in our political community—and the media is clearly a vital part of this political community.

Logan: The Martin case, as presented by the liberal (i.e., not right-wing) media, was very much a case of "low-hanging fruit." It did not represent a progressive or race-critical response to contemporary racial injustice. It involved an easy "boogeyman," an identifiably "racist" individual who shot and killed a black youth due to his "clearly held" racial prejudice. Zimmerman viewed an innocent child as "suspicious" and threatening. He may have even "uttered a racial epithet."

The activist response among non-blacks and the liberal media, in my view, was largely about righting an individual wrong. It did not involve a broader recognition of the workings of white privilege, the ways that past injustices contribute to entrenched present-day inequities, or how certain places and institutions are seen to be "white spaces." Note, in the ostensibly well-intentioned "hoodie" movement, the thousands of white activists proclaiming "I am Trayvon Martin" rather than "I am George Zimmerman." The latter statement would have implied a truer, more honest understanding of the relations of power, privilege, and economic and social violence that contribute to the devaluation of black life.

Morris: It is possible that the Trayvon Martin case will reinforce racial oppression in the United States. . . . The typical middle-class person will conclude that we, as Americans, will not stand idly by when racial wrongs occur. There will be a sense that in post-racial America [Trayvon's death was an aberration]. . . . Martin Luther King's dream is a reality. The problem is that the case will be treated as a terrible anomaly that is not deeply rooted in a reality in which black life in America is worth less than white life.

PARTICIPANT PROFILES

Charles A. Gallagher is in the departments of sociology and criminal justice at LaSalle University. He is the editor of *Rethinking the Color Line: Readings in Race and Ethnicity* (2011, McGraw-Hill), now in its fifth edition.

Zenzele Isoke is in the University of Minnesota's departments of gender, women, and sexuality studies; political science; and African American and African studies. She is the author of *Urban Black Women and the Politics of Resistance* (2013, Palgrave Macmillan).

Enid Logan is in the department of sociology at the University of Minnesota. She is the author of *"At This Defining Moment": Barack Obama's Presidential Candidacy and the New Politics of Race* (2011, NYU Press).

Aldon Morris is in the department of sociology at Northwestern University. He is the author, with Jane Mansbridge, of *Oppositional Consciousness: The Subjective Roots of Social Protest* (2001, The University of Chicago Press).

TSP tie-in

intersectionality

When it's time for that big U.S. holiday Halloween, many people jump at the opportunity to "be" someone else for a night. Unfortunately, many of the costumes they choose end up reinforcing sexist and racist stereotypes. In fact, as sociologist Lisa Wade has written on TSP Community Page Sociological Images, "[Halloween] costumes tend to collapse culturally distinct groups into a cheap stereotype." Many are offensive because they appropriate a culture's imagery, mythologizing and romanticizing groups in a way that makes their contemporary lives and struggles invisible. We can understand how these costumes are problematic by applying a logic similar to Jennifer Guiliano's in her chapter on the damage done by Native American sports mascots. Or browse thesocietypages.org/race to read a Sociological Images post by Adrienne K., a member of the Cherokee Nation of Oklahoma, who objects to such costumes because "when everyone only thinks Indians are fantasy characters put in the same category as pirates, princesses, and cartoon characters, it erases our humanity."

Not only do such costumes employ racial stereotypes, but they also often invoke stereotypes about foreign women or women of color, such as the Japanese geisha and the Indian princess, to name just a couple. This double whammy of stereotypes can be analyzed as an example of "intersectional oppression" or "intersectionality." Such examples push us to think about the overlap among different categories—race, gender, sexuality, class, nationality, or ability, for example—and how individuals or groups who belong to *multiple* oppressed groups may face *multiplied* discrimination.

So, costumes like "Pocahottie" in a fringed miniskirt and feathered headband or a Hawaiian hula girl in a grass skirt and coconut-shell bra are problematic on multiple levels. They dredge up a long history of objectifying women of color as hypersexualized and sexually available. They are also images of women of color that have associated these women with land and nature, images used to encourage settler colonialism and entice tourists for centuries. Wade writes that these women are understood as "decoration," and "treated as objects of beauty and aesthetic pleasure—exotified, in the case of 'foreign' or darker-skinned women—and used to embellish a place or experience." They are circumscribed by a web of intersectionality.

LISA GULYA

critical takes

10

american immigration and forgetting, with yen le espiritu, katherine fennelly, and douglas s. massey

STEPHEN SUH

Though the United States is known as a "melting pot," immigration has long been a divisive political and social issue here. Throughout the nation's history, countless arguments have been leveled for and against immigration practices—with numerous connections made to the nation's economy, sovereignty, and general sense of identity by both sides of the debate.

Taking these points into consideration, this roundtable discussion attempts to map the historical trajectory of immigration in the U.S. and elaborate on the multiple discourses that have surrounded it. Our panelists explain why immigration has remained an obsession for Americans, even as it was almost a nonissue in the 2012 elections.

How has the discourse regarding immigration changed over the years, if at all?

Katherine Fennelly: The question makes me think of a statement by Simon and Lynch that Americans view immigration with "rose-colored glasses turned backwards"—i.e., with positive attitudes toward earlier groups of immigrants and negative ones about those who enter today. Nevertheless, platitudes about "celebrating our heritage as a nation of immigrants" mask some of the darkest events in our nation's history, such as broad discrimination toward non-Protestant immigrants, anarchists, and others in the nineteenth century; periodic expulsions of Mexican and Chinese laborers; and the mass internment of Japanese Americans in the twentieth century. In spite of egregious examples of discrimination today, the existence of an extensive network of immigrant advocacy and human rights groups provides some counterpoint.

Yen Le Espiritu: [There is] a U.S.-immigration paradox: although the U.S. has consistently taken a restrictive approach to immigration over the years, with restrictions based mostly on race and gender, the nation has continued to represent itself as the "land of immigrants." . . . [The] moniker, as an ideological script, shores up the narrative of the United States as a nation of freedom, rights, and liberty and justice for all—an undisputed beacon for the world's "tired . . . poor . . . [and] wretched refuse." By focusing on *voluntary* immigration, this myth enables the U.S. to ideologically erase the *forcible* inclusion of indigenous groups, Mexicans, and blacks into the nation via conquest, annexation, and slavery, respectively. It also makes possible the "organized forgetting" of the fact that, since at least World War II, migration to the United States has been the product of American economic, colonial, political, and military intervention in countries around the world. Dispelling the myth of the "land of immigrants" and calling attention to the U.S. role in precipitating global migration in the first place would be an important initial step toward having an honest immigration discussion— not only locally and nationally, but also globally.

Douglas S. Massey: Over the long run, xenophobia and anti-immigrant sentiment run in cycles, usually peaking just after a period of high immigration. Today's cycle [in the U.S.] is the worst we've seen since the 1920s. It began in 1965, when the U.S. changed its laws to restrict the opportunities for legal immigration from Mexico (which, in the late 1950s, had been running at half a million per year—450,000 guest workers and 50,000 permanent residents). In 1965, the guest-worker program was terminated and permanent residence visas were capped numerically for the first time, with the cap reaching 20,000 per year in 1976. Between 1965 and 1979, the number of undocumented migrants increased rapidly until the flow of the 1950s was reestablished—except that 90% of the entries were now without authorization. The rise of "illegal" migration inspired immigration bureaucrats and conservative politicians to frame Mexican immigration as a new threat, since the migrants were illegal, so they were, by definition, "criminals" and "lawbreakers." Between 1965 and 1980, we see increased framings of immigration in the media as an invasion, a flood threatening the United States, and public opinion turns increasingly conservative and hostile to immigrants. After 1996, immigrants are increasingly conflated with terrorists and the Mexico-U.S. border becomes a symbol in the "war on terror." Hostility [toward immigrants] escalates to a peak after the economic collapse in 2008.

What about immigration allows it to remain such a fiercely debated topic within the contemporary United States?

Espiritu: Immigration policies are highly contested because they are not only instruments of border control, but also of social control. In the United States, immigration has been a technology of racialization: restrictive immigration laws have not only curtailed new arrivals but have also *produced* new racial categories such as the "excludable," the "alien" (Asian immigrants), and the "illegal" (Mexican immigrants)—categories that have outlasted the eventual repeal of these discriminatory laws. Cumulatively, these race-based policies, buttressed by popular culture, have put European and non-European immigrant groups on different trajectories of racial formation with different prospects for full membership in American society. As an example, the 1924 Johnson-Reed Act, which excluded Asians from immigration on grounds that they were racially ineligible for citizenship, cast Asians as *permanently* foreign and unassimilable. This has continued to negatively affect the group's social and cultural citizenship in the contemporary United States.

Fennelly: At its core, immigration is about nationalism, group identity, and the differentiation of "us" from "them." The positive side of nationalism promotes patriotism and a sense of pride and community solidarity; in its extreme form, nationalism breeds xenophobia and prejudice against "foreigners." This is true around the world.

Massey: Anti-immigrant groups, political opportunists, and self-interested bureaucrats are constantly pumping misinformation about immigrants and immigration into the public sphere, financed by wealthy interests who would rather see middle America mad at brown-skinned "alien invaders" than Wall Street bankers and hedge fund managers.

Aside from the DREAM Act and the hotly contested state voter ID laws, the topic of immigration seemingly took a backseat to other social and political issues in the 2012 general election. For instance, immigration was almost a nonfactor in the presidential and vice presidential debates. Why?

Massey: Romney had no interest in pursuing it, because it would lose him potential Hispanic votes, and Obama lacks the political courage to defend immigrants too forcefully.

Espiritu: Although immigration was not an explicit topic in the various debates and on the campaign trail, it certainly was present, coded most often in terms of the

"Latino vote." In the contemporary United States, the term *immigrant* has become a stand-in for *Latino immigrant*, most often for *undocumented Latino immigrant*. So I'd argue that any campaign rhetoric about the "Latino vote," both positive and negative, had an underlying immigration theme to it.

Fennelly: Immigration has been called the "third rail" of American politics. This is particularly true today, when relatively small, well-funded, right-wing groups have gained prominence and succeeded in convincing the public that immigrants pose an economic, social, and political threat to the nation. Politicians are cowed by this. At the same time, recognition of the rapid growth of Latino voters who care about immigration policies has led to a kind of stasis, in which anti- and pro-immigration groups cancel each other out.

In an increasingly transnational world, is it feasible for countries to maintain stringent border control and immigration regulations?

Massey: No, all of our efforts at control have backfired—transforming what had been a circular flow of male workers going to a handful of states into a settled population of families living in all 50 states and doubling the rate of undocumented population growth for more than a decade—all at the cost of billions of dollars of taxpayer money.

Fennelly: It is certainly feasible for governments to continue to invest in border security, in spite of its ineffectiveness. Sadly, the funding of weapons, border surveillance, and incarceration of immigrants often serves as a purposeful distraction from governments' inability to address real security threats or intractable domestic problems.

Espiritu: In any discussion on border control and immigration restriction, we have to first acknowledge the roles that the U.S. government and corporations have played— through colonialism, imperialist wars and occupations, capital investment and material extraction in Third World countries, and through active recruitment of racialized and gendered immigrant labor—in generating out-migration in the first place. In this "transnational" world, it is not only unfeasible, but also *unethical* for the U.S. to de-link its immigration policies from past U.S. corporate, military, or governmental actions abroad. As the old saying goes, "we're here because you were there."

PARTICIPANT PROFILES

Yen Le Espiritu is in the departments of sociology and ethnic studies at the University of California, San Diego. She is the author of *Home Bound: Filipino American Lives across Cultures, Communities, and Countries* (2003, University of California Press).

Katherine Fennelly is in the Humphrey School of Public Affairs at the University of Minnesota. She studies immigration, diversity, and health as they relate to public policy.

Douglas S. Massey is in the sociology department and is the director of the Office for Population Research at Princeton University. He is the author of *Brokered Boundaries: Creating Immigrant Identity in Anti-Immigrant Times* (2012, Russell Sage Foundation).

color blindness vs. race consciousness—an american ambivalence

MEGHAN A. BURKE

Consider the setting: a racially diverse urban neighborhood where organizers and most residents take a tremendous amount of pride in their community's racial diversity. But many still think the black kids in their community don't learn the "right values" and avoid the parts of the community they code as "ghetto." Or how about a rural community in Illinois, where some Tea Party organizers feel that Obama's election was a step forward for race relations, support the DREAM Act, and grew up taking pride in attending a black congregation. Those realities, taken from my own research, run counter to our expectations—the liberal, pro-diversity community should be racially conscious and committed to sustaining the diversity that they so happily embrace. And the Tea Party should be filled with seething racists who hate the president because he's black. But neither is quite accurate.

Such is the state of race and race relations in the contemporary United States. Racial diversity makes many people both proud and anxious. This ambivalence is no accident. We live in a society with deep racial inequalities and pervasive color-blind ideals. If we do not claim a critical racial consciousness—one that provides few easy answers but still has the clarity and focus to ask the difficult questions, especially those with a sharp focus on inequalities and privilege—the situation will only worsen.

color-blind ideals, deep racial inequities

In my research, I find that one of the biggest barriers to racial clarity and change is color-blind ideology—ways of talking and thinking that affirm our belief in individualism without recognizing the many remaining barriers to equality. While these are noble goals, ignoring the barriers is of little help in achieving the ideals. For example, in our K–12 curriculum, few learn about the legacies of racial inequality, and even fewer learn about the myriad forms of contemporary racism, often subtle and coded, that perpetuate inequity. We learn instead about the successes of the civil rights movement, and we gain what is often a surface-level multiculturalism, celebrating and affirming difference while avoiding acknowledgments of privilege and racism. We enact laws that formally guarantee a platform of equality and consider any "real" problems fixed. Granted, most of us can look around and see stark racial inequalities—deeply segregated neighborhoods, wealth patterned by race, unequal schools—but when all we know are the successes of the past and the grit of our own hard work, the playing field still looks level.

Color-blind ideologies are problematic because they specifically *remove* racism, past or present, as explanatory factors for disparities. If we believe that the problem is not institutional racism, and that racism is something that only *bad people* harbor in their hearts and beliefs, then we can shake our heads at the fact of inequality and still uphold the system as is. Inequality stands outside us, while we go about our day merely trying to do the right thing: valuing diversity in the abstract, claiming our own cultural heritages in ways that make us feel good, and tacitly avoiding blame or responsibility for persistent racial rifts.

My own research, conducted in the two communities alluded to in the opening, reveals not only this ambivalence, but also the identity work and social action that gets attached to it. In racially diverse urban Chicago communities, key players (block club presidents, community organizers, and other actively involved folks) proudly extol the virtues of living in a diverse community, but tend to uphold color-blind ideologies in their understanding of racial dynamics. They take pains to make clear that they are enlightened and progressive, but often make their own housing choices based on opportunity and investment. Their appreciation of diversity largely takes place through consumption—enjoying "ethnic" foods, feeling good about seeing a Pantone array of strangers' faces on the sidewalks, crafting an identity that resists the homogeneous suburbs from which many of them came. They are mostly liberal and work hard to distinguish themselves from their racist parents, relatives, coworkers, and friends. No doubt they are sincere, but their community efforts are still essentially pro-gentrification. This is not the social justice effort that is needed to eliminate racial inequalities or to sustain meaningful diversity.

The Tea Party, on the other end of the political spectrum, is not much different. My new research on organizers throughout Illinois indicates that most proudly claim color-blind stances and work hard to convey their appreciation of both diversity and fairness. They believe in the positive message that a black family in the White House sends to generations of Americans. They strongly support immigrants who came in through the "right" channels, still proudly believing this is the land of opportunity. Herman Cain, an African

American Republican presidential candidate, was the strong favorite in the straw poll at the Illinois Tea Party's regional convention in 2011, and they fear that this is becoming a country where opportunity and upward mobility are being lost. At the same time, they make use of coded racism in their lack of support for welfare and their concerns about undocumented immigration and national security—my new book is deeply critical of this racism. But, as I claim in my research, the Tea Partiers don't show any significant break from the color-blind and coded racism that I *also* found in the liberal, racially diverse community. That kind of racism is mainstream; Tea Party racism is American racism.

digging deeper into ambivalence

This racial ambivalence has a long history in the United States. It traces not only from the disconnect between racial realities and color-blind ideals but also from the pluralism of an immigrant society. In 1963, Nathan Glazer and Daniel Patrick Moynihan published *Beyond the Melting Pot*. It spoke of the reality that race and ethnicity remained salient for generations of immigrants and other marginalized populations, but overlooked the dynamics of race that had made such ethnicities optional for most whites and restrictive for most people of color. Subsequent research (notably Bob

Blauner's 1972 *Racial Oppression in America*) carefully traced the institutional dynamics of racism. Soon came lasting debates about the nature of racial inequalities in the United States, most pronounced in our collective conversations about diversity and affirmative action. Study after study has now found that most Americans support the notion of equal opportunity and diversity in the abstract, but are less willing to support actual programs and initiatives (like affirmative action, as recently addressed by the Supreme Court) and the genuine, deep engagement necessary to support multiculturalism.

Mine is not the only contemporary work to begin to unravel racial ambivalence as it unfolds into the twenty-first century. Joyce Bell and Douglas Hartmann coined the term *happy talk* in 2007 to describe the glowingly positive ways that most people talk about diversity. This positivity, they found, breaks down when respondents seek to explain how diversity operates in their everyday lives. Their interviews and analyses revealed how explicitly race-centered the discourse of diversity actually is, and how at odds it can be with Americans' beliefs in and hopes for meritocracy. Ellen Berrey has found, in one of the same communities I later studied, that a discourse focused on diversity can actually *downplay* efforts around social justice. Even scholars like Elijah Anderson can fall into the same way of thinking: In his most recent book, *The Cosmopolitan Canopy*, Anderson celebrates how diverse spaces will bring "tolerance," as though tolerance is equivalent to justice or will help sustain diversity. But who likes being merely "tolerated"?

putting privilege front and center

In 1999, sociologist Margaret Andersen wrote, "What is at issue is not so much whether the United States is a diverse society, but how to think about diversity and, fundamentally, how to conceptualize the different group experiences that comprise contemporary society." Anderson cautions against a framework that reduces race to culture—or, as she calls it, "diversity without oppression"—and goes on to explain how "losing a focus on racial inequality may be especially likely in institutional settings where there is some inclusion of diverse groups, but where the institutions remain structured on the needs and experiences of dominant groups." These days, which institutions don't meet that criteria? Politics, schools, neighborhoods, and workplaces. They all strive for diversity, but without the corresponding and necessary work of confronting the dynamics of white privilege. So the problem persists.

For that reason, recognizing and challenging privilege must be at the core of any serious discussion of diversity and inclusion. With regard to race, this means a sharp focus not only on racial inequality, but also on whiteness and white privilege. Whiteness is the cultural sensibility and collective assumptions that come to be associated with being marked as white in this society. Those categories and assumptions, like others, have a history and are constructed socially rather than biologically. Historically, being white—a category that expands and contracts with our political will—has meant the ability to be a citizen and own property, access to immigration, owning or renting in the most desirable and profitable neighborhoods, access to the best schools, and a whole host of other legal, political, and financial benefits.

Whiteness also provides individuals the "benefit of the doubt." I often tell my students that a key dynamic of white privilege in everyday life is the ability to be seen as an individual, supposedly unmarked by race, even though my own whiteness structures my day and my opportunities to the very same degree as race does for people of color. Whiteness just tends to do so in ways that benefit me. These "everyday" associations have enormous benefits for me as a white person, and they disguise the costs for people of color. Michelle Alexander, in her recent book *The New Jim Crow*, details the benefit of the doubt given to whites at every stage of the criminal justice system, with devastating consequences for people of color committing the same or lesser crimes.

race conscious, not color-blind

If we do not talk about race and diversity in ways that account for privilege, so that we can see the often-invisible workings of whiteness and be race conscious rather than color blind, racial disparities will worsen. Our current ambivalence will likely deteriorate into outright confusion, denial, or despair.

This may sound abstract, but small institutional steps are always possible. My own university has begun an innovative pre-orientation program to bring interested white students to campus at the same time as students of color and international students. Such orientations help white students focus on how they can meaningfully build community with students of different backgrounds and races on our campus and in our community. The programs also help to foster an environment in which all students can build early and honest relationships across the color line. An understanding of white privilege (owning the realities of racism in our contemporary society and taking responsibility for them) is crucial to this process. Many of the students who go through the pre-orientation shed their color-blind ideology and express gratitude for the tools that finally allow them to talk about race and privilege with confidence and competence. They go on to become leaders on campus, in their classrooms and residence halls, and in our community. It's one small step, but it works. This can and must happen in other institutions and communities.

If diversity discourse and efforts at inclusion do not include a serious and open discussion of color blindness, racism, and white privilege, including the many ways those realities intersect with other identities and oppressions, our racial ambivalence will continue. It is time to shed the ambivalence, own our racial past and present, and begin to engage the equal opportunity that so many of us in this country claim we are vested in.

RECOMMENDED READING

Margaret L. Andersen. 1999. "The Fiction of 'Diversity without Oppression'," in *Critical Ethnicity: Countering the Waves of Identity Politics*, edited by Robert H. Tai and Mary L. Kenyatta, Lanham, MD: Rowman & Littlefield. Critiques the politics of multiculturalism that do not include power and privilege.

Joyce M. Bell and Douglas Hartmann. 2007. "Diversity in Everyday Discourse: The Cultural Ambiguities and Consequences of 'Happy Talk,'" *American Sociological Review* 72(6):895–914. Demonstrates how broadly shared support for diversity dissipates in concrete settings.

Ellen C. Berrey. 2005. "Divided over Diversity: Political Discourse in a Chicago Neighborhood," *City and Community* 4(2):143–

170. Demonstrates the unintended negative consequences of a diversity-focused discourse.

Eduardo Bonilla-Silva. 2012 [2003]. *Racism without Racists: Color-Blind Racism and the Persistence of Racial Inequality in the United States*, Lanham, MD: Rowman & Littlefield. Explores the patterned ways that we uphold color-blind ideology in everyday discussions about race.

exposing *the new jim crow* with michelle alexander

KIA HEISE

Michelle Alexander made a shocking claim in her 2010 book *The New Jim Crow*: in the wake of the civil rights era, she argues, criminal punishment has come to succeed slavery and legal discrimination as a powerful and comprehensive system of racial control in the United States. As a civil rights lawyer and law professor, Alexander assembled decades of social science evidence in building a strong and convincing case for her provocative claim. The book quickly became a bestseller, inspiring students, prisoners, policy makers, and readers from all walks of life. It also spawned a social movement to challenge racialized mass incarceration and the relegation of felons to second-class citizenship. TSP spoke with Alexander about exposing—and pushing back against—carceral control.

Kia Heise: Why do you think mass incarceration and the criminal justice system should be such central topics in any discussion of race?

Michelle Alexander: In my view, the mass incarceration of poor people of color is the most pressing racial justice issue of our time. I think there is a tremendous amount of mythology regarding the explosion in our criminal justice system. In my experience, most people *imagine* that our prison population quintupled in the United States and millions of black and brown people began cycling in and out of prison due largely to bad schools, broken homes, and poverty. But, what I came to learn in my years of work and research on these issues is that the conventional explanations and justifications for our prison explosion are simply wrong. Our prison population did not explode simply because of crime or crime rates; it can't be explained by failing schools or poverty.

Crime rates over the past few decades have fluctuated, fallen, and we've had bad schools and high levels of poverty in poor communities of color forever! But we've never had a system of mass incarceration like this one. And this system of mass incarceration has fundamentally altered the life course for millions of people in the United States and created a caste-like system in many communities.

People are trapped, literally from cradle to grave, born into a system in which they are targeted by police at young ages and swept into the criminal justice system (primarily for non-violent and drug-related crimes—the very sorts of crimes that occur with roughly equal frequency in middle-class, white communities and college campuses, but are largely ignored). They're swept in, branded "criminals" and "felons," and then stripped of the very rights supposedly won in the civil rights movement era— the right to vote, the right to serve on juries, and the right to be free of legal discrimination in employment, housing, access to education, and public benefits. *So* many of the old forms of discrimination that we supposedly left behind during the old Jim Crow era are suddenly legal again once you've been branded a criminal or a felon.

The scale of mass incarceration, I think, goes beyond what most people even realize. Prisons are "out of sight and out of mind" for those who are not directly impacted; most people have no idea of the millions who are now trapped in a permanent second-class status, many of whom are cycling in and out of prisons and jails, unable to find work or housing because of the legal discrimination they face. These millions are trapped in a cycle of perpetual marginality. This system of racial and social control is eerily reminiscent of an era that we've supposedly left behind.

And it's *easy* to justify each form of discrimination one by one. It's easy to make rational arguments about *why* one form of discrimination might make sense. But then, when you put them all together, you see that there is a web that does operate to trap people, often for relatively minor offenses. They're forced to pay for their mistakes for the rest of their lives.

Heise: What sort of grassroots movement did it take to get this conversation going when you published *The New Jim Crow*?

Alexander: Well, first I should point out that my book didn't strike much interest in the beginning. During the first year, I couldn't get anybody to review the book; I had trouble finding anyone who would want me to come speak. The book was released literally the same month that Obama was inaugurated for the first time, and I remember that when I was finishing the book, doing my final revisions, Obama was on the campaign trail in the primaries, running against Hillary. I remember thinking to myself, "If Obama wins the presidency, no one is going to buy the idea that we have something like a caste system existing in the United States today!"

I thought, "It's going to make it impossible for this message to be heard." And it was true for the first year. The media was awash in "post-racial" sentiment, and it was very difficult to have this conversation about something like a racial caste system still existing in the United States. But after the initial "Obama euphoria" began to wear off, there was an opening where people were starting to reflect a little more carefully on, "What does the Obama presidency really mean? How far have we really come?"

That created an opening for deeper reflection. I should also say that I don't think the book would have really launched if it hadn't been for a very small, non-profit, grassroots organization based in Chicago called The Black Star Project. It's an organization dedicated to closing the achievement gap between kids of color and white kids, achieving educational equity in inner-city schools. They don't even do any work around criminal justice reform, but the executive director of that organization, Phillip Jackson, read the book and called me up. He basically said, "We need, people need to hear this in Chicago. All of the students, all of the parents we work with, we're living this reality. We have entire communities that are under correctional control. The parents of these kids are cycling in and out of prisons and jails, and no one understands what's really going on. Everyone just suspects that something is horribly awry, but there's just a lot of shaming and blaming that occurs within our own communities. People need to understand. Come and speak."

And so he invited me to come and speak at a church in Chicago, and he packed that church with hundreds of people, videotaped my speech (which was very well received), then sent out probably 20 different e-mails to tens of thousands of people on his listserv with clips of my speeches, just telling people, "You have to read this book. You have to read this book. You have to invite her to speak." And he has an enormous network, and it's one of these stories of the miracles of social networking, where all of a sudden I started receiving requests to come speak from all over the country.

It started off with churches and community groups, and then I started getting requests from schools and momentum began to build. I finally got asked to do some mainstream media interviews and the ball began to roll.

But I really trace it to, you know, one small organization taking it upon itself to really launch a crusade to raise consciousness around these issues and connect the dots between what people who were working on education reform and education equity were doing to the work of people who are fighting to end mass incarceration.

Heise: What's been the reaction to your argument—positive or resistant?

Alexander: Overwhelmingly, people are positive and want very much to take action. As I travel around the country, the question that comes up over and over again is "What now? What do we do? What does it really mean to build a movement to end mass incarceration, and what can I, as an ordinary person or a student or an academic, what can I do to build this movement and contribute to this work?"

One of my frustrations has been that there is no national, grassroots organization dedicated to ending mass incarceration. During the Jim Crow era, there was an organization: the NAACP, a grassroots organization with chapters around the country dedicated to ending Jim Crow. During slavery, there were abolitionist organizations that were grassroots, dedicated to ending slavery. The list can go on of examples where it's necessary to make a major shift not just in policy, but a *cultural* shift, and that requires a shift in public consciousness at a grassroots level. Any effort to end mass incarceration *requires* that there's some kind of national organization rooted in communities, helping to move the work and the agenda forward and to force dialogue in communities around our country. And that doesn't exist yet.

So it's very difficult to tell those who want to get involved what exactly to do. There is no one organization just focused on this like a laser. I am really encouraged by the fact that around the country, Students Against Mass Incarceration chapters are beginning to form on college campuses and universities. The first one was born at Howard University, but now I think that there are a dozen or more different chapters. I think this year they're having their first national conference . . . [they are] struggling to find their voice in this time, thinking about what strategies and tactics are necessary to raise awareness and engage in a movement for real change.

And the faith community, for the first time, is beginning to really organize against mass incarceration. So there are lots of hopeful signs, but I think we still have a ways to go before we reach a point where it'll be easy—or much easier—to tell people in any given community what they can do to connect to the movement.

Heise: You critique the notion of "color blindness" in your work. For many Americans (especially white Americans), it can take quite a psychological jump to abandon everything they've been taught or that they want to believe about this promise of color blindness. How does this ideal of "not seeing race" stand in opposition to what you're trying to advocate?

Alexander: What I've tried to argue in the book and elsewhere is that "blindness" is really just the wrong metaphor for what ought to be our goal in working toward a more just and inclusive society. What we've seen over the last few decades is that our nation has not so much become blind to *race* (of course, we still see our racial differences and the color of each other's skin and we notice race); we've become blind to *racial suffering.* We've become blind to the experiences and basic humanity of people of different racial and ethnic groups. I really believe that our goal isn't to work toward blindness and indifference toward one another—to not "see" race—but toward seeing race and *still* caring about the person you see. . . . We want to be able to see discrimination and racial disparities and see racial injustice when it occurs and *respond* to it with care, compassion, and concern.

But this mentality of "color blindness" has encouraged us, instead, to adopt an attitude of "I don't care if he's black. I don't care what race he or she is." And to rationalize this mentality of color blindness allows us to rationalize our indifference to . . . the experiences of groups of people defined by race.

We don't need to be blind to one another in order to care about one another. In fact, the more we insist upon being blind and not seeing each other fully as we are, the more likely it is that we will be able to rationalize our indifference, close our eyes to the actual lived experiences of others.

Heise: How does the problem of mass incarceration—*racialized* mass incarceration—start to get addressed within a white-dominated society that may not think this is *their* problem?

Alexander: I think it really goes to the core challenges of building a movement against mass incarceration: how do we inspire people to care about those who seem different on the surface (they look different, they're "the other")? How do we inspire people to care about the other, especially when the other has been labeled as a criminal?

There is no clear self-interest at stake, and that dilemma has led many civil rights advocates and policy reformers to believe that we have to talk to white audiences about the costs of mass incarceration and make it clear that . . . it's hitting their pocketbooks in ways that they may not realize. If they want to save money, if they want a less expensive way of managing crime and punishment in the United States, they need to think about doing things differently.

I can see why people are tempted by that strategy of simply appealing—or trying to appeal—to white self-interest, but my own view is that the strategy will fail in the long run. There really is no getting around the need to begin to define and adopt strategies and language that will challenge more privileged communities (along lines of race and class and ethnicity) to *care* about the others simply because they share a common humanity.

That was the genius of the civil rights movement: the tactics of creative non-violence and the message of the movement challenged people to imagine that they had a shared humanity with those they viewed as different or "other" or inferior. The tactics themselves *forced* a public conversation. They helped to make visible what was hidden or denied. Just as prisons today are "out of sight, out of mind," during the old Jim Crow era, the caste system wasn't out of sight, but it was out of mind. It was easy for people to rationalize the whole way of being. . . . With the Montgomery bus boycott and the Freedom Rides, the tactics that were employed, especially because they *invited* so much hostility and resistance, helped to dramatize the injustice and force the public conversation.

There's a wonderful essay that I highly recommend called "Bleeding Heart" by Tom Stoddard, the former director of LAMBDA. . . . The thesis of the article is that advocates, people who are working for social change, have to determine at the outset whether they are seeking simply *rule shifting* (like a change in a law here or there) or *cultural transformation*. If the goal is cultural transformation (if the ultimate goal is shifting the way people think and how they relate to one another and society as a whole), then nothing short of a major movement that involves a major conflict over values—basically, a big public fight—has any hope of success.

I share Stoddard's view. I think piecemeal policy reform efforts are important, but ultimately we're going to have to figure out how to force a public conversation about what we, as a nation, have done *again* by creating this massive system of incarceration, a penal system unprecedented in human history. We're going to have to force a public conversation about [the caste system we've created with mass incarceration] and make sure that our strategies and tactics are conducive to inspiring people to imagine a shared humanity, a common humanity.

So, it's no easy task, but it's been done before, and I believe, with some courage, we can do it again. I'm inspired by work that I see going on in communities all over the country right now. We'll find our way sooner or later.

PARTICIPANT PROFILE

Michelle Alexander is a civil rights lawyer, advocate, and scholar. She is in the Kirwin Institute for the Study of Race and Ethnicity and the Moritz College of Law at The Ohio State University.

TSP tie-in

an experiment in black and white

I n the TSP roundtable "Thinking about Trayvon," featured in this book, the panelists emphasize how, in the United States, many have difficulty seeing black males as anything but suspicious, threatening, and in need of containment and discipline. Sociologists Matthew Desmond and Mustafa Emirbayer, along with many others, even argue that the stigmatizing of blacks as criminals is so deeply entrenched in America's collective consciousness that the fear of crime has more to do with fear of blackness than with crime itself.

In a dramatic illustration, two segments from the ABC news series *What Would You Do?* (browse thesocietypages .org/race to watch the clip) show how social and cultural associations between blackness and criminality manifest in day-to-day life. In one segment, a group of black male teens and a group of white male teens dressed in similar clothing vandalize a car in broad daylight in a predominately white suburban park. In the other segment, one white male and one black male try to steal a locked bike in another busy park. In both cases, the mostly white park-goers are much more likely to directly confront, criticize, and call the police on the black vandals. Further, while the ABC crew filmed their group of white actors vandalizing the car, 9-1-1 actually got more calls about another suspicious group: some black actors the show had left "sleeping" in another car!

The public's responses show just how deeply internalized assumptions about blackness, deviance, and crime are related to disparate rates of arrests, police surveillance, and incarceration among black Americans. The 9-1-1 calls speak to how many black youth are often under surveillance by more than just law enforcement agents: they are subject to strict social control. The stringent civilian surveillance demonstrates that even in public spaces, black youth are assumed to be "out of place" and criminal threats.

ABC's experiment lets those who aren't black see how conceptions about blackness and criminality influence what behavior is seen as "deviant." But, as one student pointed out in the comments section of TSP's Community Page Sociological Images, many who watch the video and most of the bystanders ABC interviewed insisted that they did not consider race in their response to the staged crimes. The ease with which these people can claim "color blindness" highlights the degree to which Meghan Burke's call in this volume for "race consciousness" is needed.

ALEX MANNING

diversity and
the new CEOs

RICHARD L. ZWEIGENHAFT AND
G. WILLIAM DOMHOFF

Twenty years ago we wrote a book about African American teenagers from low-income backgrounds who went to elite boarding schools through a program called A Better Chance. We predicted: "It seems unlikely that more than two or three blacks will make it to the very top of a Fortune 1000 company in the next two decades, even with the cultural capital of prep school and Ivy League educations." We were wrong. By spring 2011, 14 African Americans had become CEOs at Fortune 500 companies.

The trend moved rather quickly. When the first edition of our book, *Diversity in the Power Elite*, came out in 1998, we had to look at corporate directors, not CEOs, as there just wasn't enough diversity among CEOs to study. By the second edition, eight years later, there were 46 women and people of color in the corner office of top firms. Indeed, every few months, a Fortune 500 corporation appoints a CEO who is not a white male—that is, they select one of what we call "the New CEOs." In October 2011, IBM tapped Virginia Rometty, a white woman; in late March 2012, McDonald's chose Don Thompson, an African American male; and in early April 2012, Avon announced Sherilyn McCoy, a white woman, would replace Andrea Jung, the Chinese American woman who had been its CEO since 1998. With McCoy's appointment, the tally of the New CEOs at Fortune 500 companies stood at 80 white women, African Americans, Latinos, and Asian Americans.

As we consider these changes, we are especially intrigued by the appointments of the first two African American CEOs of Fortune 500 companies in 1999, the subsequent appointments of 12 more by the time our book *The New CEOs* came out in 2011, and now one more in 2012 (Thompson at McDonalds). *The New CEOs* considered the group of 14 African Americans, 25 white women, 15 Latinos, and 20 Asian Americans just about every which way, including background (in terms of geography, class, and education), skin color, whether they were internal or external hires, their pay, which politicians they have supported, which companies appointed them, and whether those companies are rated positively by organizations and magazines like the Human Rights Campaign, the National Organization for Working Mothers, *Fortune*, and *Working Mother*, each of which rates corporations on good "corporate citizenship" and fair treatment of women and gay, lesbian, and transgender employees. We asked why there had been such an increase in CEO diversity even in the years of George W. Bush's presidency. What could we learn about diversity and the power elite?

Here, with another year of information to draw upon, we look at the New CEOs in terms of class and gender, using an intersectional analysis to help explain who becomes a New CEO—and who does not.

assessing class and other differences

It's very difficult to know a person's wealth (or background of wealth), but, as various sociologists and economists have shown, wealth is a crucial predictor of life chances—better, even, than annual income. In the case of CEOs, it is especially difficult because they and their publicists go out of their way to be misleading: all CEOs, it seems, worked their way up from the bottom. Consider, for example, Carly Fiorina, the former CEO of Hewlett-Packard and 2010 Republican Senate nominee in California. She is said to embody the American Dream, having climbed the corporate ladder from humble beginnings. In her memoir, *Tough Choices*, she writes of her "modest, middle-class family." When she campaigned with

John McCain in his 2008 presidential bid, he introduced her over and over again by telling audiences she "began as a part-time secretary." In reality, Fiorina grew up a child of privilege. By her own account, before he became a federal judge, her father taught law at the University of Texas, Cornell, Yale, Stanford, and Duke; his sabbaticals took the family around the world, including one stop in London where she attended the posh-sounding Channing School for Select Young Ladies. At four, she was already taking French lessons and going to the opera. She may very well have been a part-time secretary, but to suggest that she moved from anywhere near the bottom of the class structure to the top is a bedtime story.

So, to assess the class backgrounds of the New CEOs, we did what sociologists usually do—we used the best information available to determine their parents' (and sometimes grandparents') occupations and educational levels. Among the white women, we concluded about 70% came from upper-middle or upper-class families (that is, the top 15% of the class structure). The 70% figure closely follows estimates made by other academics who have systematically studied the class backgrounds of top corporate executives. Similarly, a look at the Latino CEOs, all of whom have been male and most of whom were born and raised outside the United States, shows about two-thirds came from upper-middle or upper-class families.

Among the 20 Asian American Fortune 500 CEOs (a fairly loose category that included not only Japanese and Chinese Americans, but also eight CEOs who were born in India, one in Sri Lanka, and one in Pakistan; just one-quarter of the Asian American CEOs were born in the United States, but most have become American citizens), we concluded that most were from the upper-middle or upper classes of the countries in which they grew up. Three of the Asian Americans are women: Andrea Jung, CEO of Avon from 1999 until just recently; Indra Nooyi, CEO of PepsiCo since 2006; and Laura Sen, CEO of BJ's Wholesale Club since 2009. Despite Jung's claim that her Chinese immigrant parents "had nothing when they came here," her father was an architect and her mother a chemical engineer. Even if they came without economic capital, they came with cultural capital, including advanced education and valuable occupational experience. Jung went to Princeton, where she majored in English literature. Nooyi, whose father was a banker and whose aunt was a noted classical musician, came to study at Yale after graduating from college in India, and at one time described herself as "a good, conservative, south Indian Brahmin girl." Sen's Chinese father was a highway engineer; her Irish mother worked as a secretary.

Only the 14 African American CEOs break the pattern: most are not from economically privileged families. More typically, as is the case for Richard Parsons, former CEO of Time Warner and until recently the chair of Citi, they come from working-class families in which money was tight, but they did not grow up thinking they were poor (Parsons explained in one interview, "When I was a kid . . . I had absolutely no idea that we were statistically working poor. We were like everyone else on the block; it didn't seem so bad to me"). Though some, like Kenneth Chenault, CEO of American Express since 2001, came from professional families that were well-off (his father was a dentist), many grew up with parents who were factory workers, postmen, custodians, daycare workers, or house cleaners. The single African American woman in this group, Ursula Burns (CEO of Xerox since 2009), was raised by a single mother who took in ironing.

With the exception of the African Americans among them, the New CEOs share the same class backgrounds as the "Old CEOs"—the white men who previously held these positions and still make up 93% of the Fortune 500 CEOs. The white women CEOs certainly are similar in terms of class background to the white male CEOs, as are the Latinos and the Asian Americans.

Almost 15 years ago, when we looked at the women who had served as corporate directors of Fortune 500 companies, we found that they were better educated than their white male counterparts. They were more likely to have attended elite colleges and universities and to have earned postgraduate degrees. The same pattern holds for the women CEOs. These findings support the oft-asserted claim that in order to advance in a world that discriminates, women (and other groups facing such discrimination) have to be better educated and perform better than their white male competition. The exceptions, however, reveal the importance of scholarship programs that allow those from the lower rungs of the class structure to attend elite boarding schools, excellent undergraduate colleges and universities, and graduate schools. For example, after a stellar career at a public high school in Seattle that included serving as student body president and quarterbacking the football team, Franklin Raines, the former CEO of Fannie Mae, won a Harvard scholarship. After attending Catholic schools and NYU, Xerox's Ursula Burns won a fellowship (paid for by Xerox) that covered her graduate school education at Columbia University. These exceptions to the general rule (that class privilege is key to one's chances of becoming a CEO) demonstrate the importance of scholarships and other educational aid.

playing the corporate game

When we first looked at the experiences of women in the corporate world, we found that many complained about issues related to golf. Women executives told researchers and journalists that the amount of business taking place on the "back 9" put them at a disadvantage. Hazel O'Leary, a former corporate executive who became Secretary of Energy in the Clinton administration, told an interviewer that she felt she had to take up the sport. "Without losing your own personality," she explained, "it's important to be part of the prevailing culture. At this company it's golf. I've resisted learning to play golf all my life but I finally had to admit I was missing something that way."

Golf remains an issue today: even if women learn how to play, they may not be included, and some courses don't allow them anyway. Lloyd Ward, one of the African American CEOs on our list (he was CEO of Maytag from 1999 to 2000), took some heat when it was revealed that he was one of the few African American members of the Augusta Country Club, home of the Masters Golf Tournament and a club that continued to bar women from membership until August of 2012. More recently, Augusta's policy came under scrutiny because IBM sponsors the Masters Tournament—IBM's own CEO, a woman, wouldn't be allowed to play there. Aylwin Lewis, another of the African American Fortune 500 CEOs (Kmart/Sears, from 2004 to 2008), at one point issued a decree that, at his company, there could be no discussion of business matters on the golf course. He refused to leave important company players out of the loop just because they were not golfers (or were not invited to play).

Going further, many have argued that because women have had fewer opportunities to participate in organized team sports (and, thus, to learn the leadership skills, teamwork, and other character-building attributes allegedly tied to participation in organized sports), they have been disadvantaged in the corporate world. This may be. We did find some younger women CEOs who'd grown up with Title IX and played competitive sports in high school and college. For example, Meg Whitman, former CEO of eBay and current CEO of Hewlett-Packard, played field hockey and lacrosse in high school and at Princeton. But, here again, class and education intersect with opportunity. How does one learn to play golf, field hockey, or lacrosse? For a host of reasons, including the costs of playing these sports and the necessary time investments by kids and their parents, a disproportionate number of those who play certain sports hail from the privileged classes or had scholarships to tony private schools, and they are less likely to have played what are sometimes called "prole" (or "proletarian") sports like basketball. We did find that many of the African American male CEOs—the one group of New CEOs, you will recall, that did not tend to come from privilege—had played "prole" sports at the high school or college level, but that crucial intersection of class, education, and gender seems to have effectively kept both women and those from the lower classes from participating in upper-crust sports or gaining the social capital such sporting networks might provide.

learning from the pipeline

How will class, education, gender, and other factors help shape future appointments of white women, African Americans, Latinos, and Asian Americans as Fortune-level CEOs? We looked at some key points in the executive pipeline that typically are part of the path to the corner office: graduating from college, earning MBA or law degrees, earning more than $250,000 per year, and, probably most importantly, attaining a senior executive position in a Fortune 500 company that is just one step from the CEO office. The first three of those indicators are available as part of national data sets. To check on the last, we looked up Fortune 500 companies online and used photos of the "management team," "executive team," "senior leadership committee," or other groups of senior-most executives. With two separate student opinions as to the distribution of women, African Americans, Latinos, and Asian Americans in photos of 3,072 individuals across 262 companies, we concluded that about two-thirds of those a step from the CEO office were white men, about 19% were white women, slightly fewer than 3% were African Americans, about 4% were Latinos, and about 8% were Asian Americans (see the figure below).

These data place the much-smaller percentages of women CEOs of color in stark relief: there are no such differences earlier in the executive pipeline. In fact, far more African American women earn college degrees, MBAs, and law degrees than African American men, and about as many Latinas and Asian American women earn these degrees as Latinos and Asian American men. However, when we look at the steps that approach the CEO office more closely (those earning $250,000 a year and those just one step from the CEO office), women of color almost disappear.

Individuals One Step from CEO

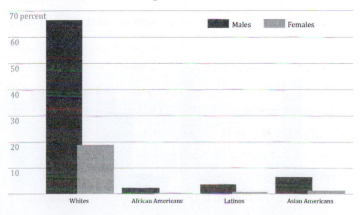

To show this more clearly, in the figure below we have summarized the ratios of men to women for each of four potential steps to the CEO office. With the exception of African Americans, the ratios are not too high either in favor of men or women for the first two categories, but they diverge in the third and fourth steps: that is, men are much more likely to earn those big salaries and much more likely to be one step from the CEO office. In that last, most important category, the male-to-female ratio is highest for the three ethnic groups (African American, Latino, and Asian American), with men much more likely to hold such positions than women.

In one of our earlier books, we argued that, in order to make it through the diversity gauntlet, an aspiring non–white male

Pathways to CEO: Ratios of Males to Females

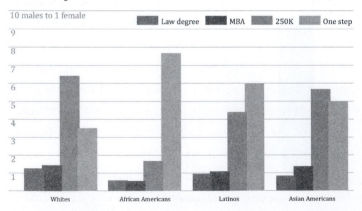

executive could not be too different from the white males who made up, and still make up, the majority of the power elite. It was as if the diversifiers lost points, so to speak, for each category of difference. For example, a black male lost one point, but a black female lost two points. It's a crude numerical way of saying, as social psychology studies reveal, that in-groupers look for commonality when they consider bringing in allies from among traditional out-groups. But even white males could lose points for having dreadlocks or wearing a yarmulke.

Back in the 1980s, in an interview study of executives who had received MBAs from Harvard Business School, female Jewish executives all agreed that being female was more of an impediment to their careers than being a Jew, but many quickly emphasized that being Jewish, or different in any other way, was not irrelevant. As one put it, "It's the whole package. I heard secondhand from someone as to how I would be perceived as a pushy, Jewish broad who went and got an MBA. Both elements, being Jewish and being a woman, together with having the MBA, were combined to create a stereotype I had to work against from the first day." Another woman explained, "It's part of the question of whether you fit the mold. Are you like me or not? If too much doesn't fit, it impacts you negatively." Our current findings suggest that this becomes increasingly apparent the closer one gets to the CEO office.

With this kind of a crude metric in mind, it is not surprising that there have been far more white women CEOs (26 and counting) than African American women CEOs (1), Asian American women CEOs (3), or Latino women CEOs (none). The data we've gathered showing who is one step from the CEO office lead us to conclude that these patterns will continue. Culture (in the form of cultural capital), education, and class are all still in play. While gender and color remain the best predictors of who will make it into the upper echelons of the corporate world, beyond that, it's intersectionality wherever we look.

RECOMMENDED READING

Denise Benoit. 2007. *The Best-Kept Secret: Women Corporate Lobbyists, Policy, & Power in the United States,* Rutgers, NJ: Rutgers University Press. Shows how women with expertise in finance and taxes became useful to corporations that wanted to maintain access to Congress, especially when more women became important members of the legislative process as elected officials and staff members of finance committees.

Sharon M. Collins. 1997. *Black Corporate Executives: The Making and Breaking of a Black Middle Class,* Philadelphia, PA: Temple University Press. An in-depth look at the experiences of black corporate executives before there were any black CEOs.

Dennis Gilbert. 2011. *The American Class Structure in an Age of Growing Inequality* (8th edition), Thousand Oaks, CA: SAGE. Provides a valuable model for understanding class in America.

C. Wright Mills. 2000 [1956]. *The Power Elite,* New York: Oxford University Press. A classic that shows the absence of diversity in the highest circles of the corporate, political, and military worlds in the 1950s. Mills was more focused on the over-representation of those from the highest classes than the under-representation of women and people of color.

Thomas M. Shapiro and Melvin L. Oliver. 2006. *Black Wealth–White Wealth* (2nd edition), New York: Routledge. Not only are there black-white wealth gaps, but they are growing. This book explores the hidden costs of being African American that perpetuate inequality.

discussion guide
and group activities

discussion guide

1. Sociologists often talk about race as a "social construction"—that is, a social category that is not natural or physiological, but "made" in and through human activity. Use two or three chapters from this volume to identify key insights or evidence that illustrate the social construction of race. Why is this way of thinking about race so important to sociologists?

2. How can images and representations of black men—often among the most egregious and troubling in American culture—help explain the persistent racial homicide gap described by Lauren Krivo and Julie Phillips in Chapter 2? Use the interviews with Michelle Alexander and the roundtable on media discourses about Trayvon Martin to support and develop your points.

3. Not all racial stereotypes are created equal. How does the "stereotype promise" described by Jennifer Lee in

Chapter 3 differ from the "stereotype threat" that other people of color face?

4. In Chapter 7, Jennifer Guiliano describes the history of sport mascots using Native American themes. Browse thesocietypages.org/race to see a collection of Native American mascot images, then compare them to stereotypes used to characterize black athletes. Do you view these images differently than you did before? Why do you think these mascots have been difficult to ban from college and professional sports?

5. We often think of prejudice, racial stereotypes, and racism as relics from the past, now held only by the worst, most intolerant people in society. How do Chapters 5 and 12, featuring Matthew Hughey and Michelle Alexander, challenge these understandings of prejudice and discrimination?

6. Chapters 1, 4, and 10 all address how immigration continues to change racial boundaries and categories in the United States. How, in particular, does Wendy Roth's chapter on Latino identity illustrate immigration's effects on racial identification?

7. Browse thesocietypages.org/race to watch a video on how changing racial demographics might affect electoral politics in the United States. How does the video add to what you learned in this volume, particularly as it relates to Chapters 1, 4, and 11?

8. One of the challenges of studying race and racism is how they can exert their influence even in cultural realms we see as "raceless." How do the chapters on the environment, crime, sports, and mass media show racism and racial disparities operating in unexpected places? Choose another sphere (say, religion or pop music) and talk with your group about how race operates in it.

9. Create a list of five social facts found in this book and on our website that help us understand the challenges faced by people of color who want to become the "new CEOs," as discussed by Richard Zweigenhaft and G. William Domhoff in Chapter 13.

10. What is the ideology of "color blindness" and why is it so appealing to many Americans? Why do many scholars believe it actually perpetuates racial inequality? Use Chapters 11 and 12 to inform your discussion.

11. Browse thesocietypages.org/race to read a Sociological Images post about how companies use racial stereotypes to advertise during Black History Month. How does author Lisa Wade's conclusion echo Meghan Burke's argument in Chapter 11? Thinking about the diversity program Burke describes for undergraduates at her university, what are some other ways systematic racism can be undermined with race consciousness? Also consider Chapter 12 and *The New Jim Crow*.

group activities

ACTIVITY 1: WHITE PRIVILEGE KNAPSACK

To explain white privilege, many turn to the classic piece "White Privilege: Unpacking the Invisible Knapsack" by Peggy McIntosh. Since some people might dismiss McIntosh's article as "outdated" (it was written in 1988), this activity encourages readers to update the activity so that it fits with current race relations. First, discussion group members update McIntosh's examples to match modern social patterns, then they add new examples of white privilege to the list to round out the scope of their awareness around systemic racial discrimination.

Part 1

After reading "Unpacking the Invisible Knapsack" (readily available online), the group's members should split into a few pairs or small groups, each of which will have a list of 8 of the 26 privileges McIntosh identifies. Working together, the group should select "outdated" items, aiming to find at least one outdated privilege to discuss with the full group, as well as one that still seems prevalent. How would the discussants change each item to update it? When the group reconvenes, they should consider whether the privileges have been amplified (that is, have become stronger) or faded away. How have other privileges affected, replaced, or erased the "outdated" privileges?

Part 2

Each discussant should now take a few minutes to consider a racial privilege not yet noted on the list and explain how he or she has seen this privilege in action. If this is difficult, ask the group to share a recent experience in interviewing for a job, an interaction with an authority figure like a police officer, or making a major purchase like a computer, house, or car.

ACTIVITY 2: RACE, ETHNICITY, AND THE CENSUS

Is "Latino" a race or an ethnicity? Wendy Roth tackles this question in Chapter 4. Hand out an example of the Census questions on the respondents' race and ethnicity (browse thesocietypages.org/race for an example). Everyone should fill in the form, then discuss the following questions (break into smaller groups if your reading group is more than a few people):

1. Do the available categories on this form line up with your own racial and ethnic identity? Why or why not?

2. Are there better ways to classify people racially? How would you edit this form?

3. Does listing "Hispanic" as an ethnicity, but not a race, make sense? Why or why not?

4. What are some benefits and drawbacks to listing "Hispanic" as an ethnicity?

5. Why is the Latino race/ethnicity question a controversial topic? Would a consensus on "ethnicity" or "race" change anything for Latino Americans or the U.S. government? What about for other Americans' notions of racial categories?

about the contributors

Meghan A. Burke is in the department of sociology at Illinois Wesleyan University. She is the author of *Racial Ambivalence in Diverse Communities: Whiteness and the Power of Color-Blind Ideologies* (2012, Lexington Books).

G. William Domhoff is in the department of sociology at the University of California at Santa Cruz. He is the author of *Who Rules America?* (now in its seventh edition, published by McGraw-Hill in 2013).

Jennifer Guiliano is the assistant director of the Maryland Institute for Technology in the Humanities and is coauthor with Simon Appleford of DevDH.org, a resource for digital humanities project development.

Lisa Gulya is in the sociology program at the University of Minnesota and is a member of The Society Pages' graduate editorial board. She studies family, reproduction, and social policy.

Douglas Hartmann is in the department of sociology at the University of Minnesota. His research interests focus on race and ethnicity, multiculturalism, popular culture (including sports and religion), and contemporary American society. He is coeditor of The Society Pages.

Kia Heise is in the sociology program at the University of Minnesota. She studies social movements and race relations.

Matthew W. Hughey is in the department of sociology at the University of Connecticut. He is the author of *White Bound: Nationalists, Antiracists, and the Shared Meanings of Race* (2012, Stanford University Press).

Lauren J. Krivo is in the sociology department and is affiliated with the Criminal Justice Program at Rutgers University. She is the author, with Ruth D. Peterson, of *Divergent Social Worlds: Neighborhood Crime and the Racial-Spatial Divide* (2010, Russell Sage).

Jennifer Lee is in the sociology department at the University of California at Irvine and was a Russell Sage Foundation Visiting Scholar for 2011–2012.

Alex Manning is in the sociology program at the University of Minnesota. He studies race, sports, and youth development.

Hollie Nyseth Brehm is a PhD candidate in sociology at the University of Minnesota. She studies human rights, international crime, representations of atrocities, and environmental sociology. She is an NSF Graduate Research Fellow and the graduate editor of The Society Pages.

David N. Pellow is in the sociology department at the University of Minnesota. He is the author, with Lisa Sun-Hee Park, of *The Slums of Aspen: Immigrants vs. the Environment in America's Eden* (2011, New York University Press).

Julie A. Phillips is in the sociology department and the Institute for Health, Health Care Policy, and Aging Research at Rutgers University. She studies the causes and consequences of various forms of social inequality.

Wendy Roth is in the department of sociology at the University of British Columbia. She is the author of *Race Migrations: Latinos and the Cultural Transformation of Race* (2012, Stanford University Press).

Stephen Suh is in the sociology program at the University of Minnesota. He studies race and ethnicity.

Christopher Uggen is a sociologist and criminologist at the University of Minnesota. He believes that good science can light the way to a more just and safer world. He is coeditor of The Society Pages.

Matt Wray is in the department of sociology at Temple University. He is the author of *Cultural Sociology: An Introductory Reader* (2013, W. W. Norton).

Wing Young Huie is an award-winning documentary photographer and author in Minneapolis, Minnesota.

Richard L. Zweigenhaft is in the department of psychology at Guilford College. He is the author, with G. William Domhoff, of *The New CEOs* (2011, Rowman & Littlefield).

index

affirmative action programs,
16–17, 170
African Americans
diversity and new CEOs, 192,
195–96, 198, 200–203
environmental inequality and,
116–20, 123
homicide victimization rates,
21–24
interracial marriages and, 13
music and, 76–77
poverty and, 12
racial categories and, 46
SAT scores and college
admissions, 42
shifting color lines, 10
socioeconomic status, 69
sports mascots and, 98–99
stereotype threat and, 38
white trash term and, 85
Alba, Richard, 4–6
Alexander, Michelle, xxiii, 172,
177–88
All-Weather Illiberals, 66–67

All-Weather Liberals, 66–67
Andersen, Margaret, 171
Anderson, Elijah, 170–71
AP (Advanced Placement) track
(school), 31, 33, 35, 37
Arnold, Tom, 84
Asian Americans
demographic trends, 3
demolition derby example,
xxv–xxviii
diversity and new CEOs, 192,
195, 200–203
environmental inequality and,
123
exceptionalism, 40–43
homicide victimization
rates, 25
immigration trends, 8
interracial marriages and, 13
Linsanity phenomenon,
27–28
poverty and, 12
racial categories and, 46
racial identity and, 62

Asian Americans (*continued*)
  recommended reading, 43–44
  SAT scores and college
    admissions, 42–43
  self-fulfilling prophecy, 29,
    35–37
  shifting color lines and, 9–10
  stereotype promise, 29,
    37–41
  stereotype threat, 29, 38
  success frame for, 28–29, 34–35
  symbolic capital, 29–35
Asian tax, 42
assimilation
  of immigrants, 5–6, 11–12
  racial identity and, 59–60
  segmented, 10–11
Audre Lorde Project, 139

Barr, Roseanne, 84
Beck, Glenn, 15
Beck, Ulrich, 122
Bell, Buck v., 89–90
Bell, Joyce, xxvii, 170
Bender, Charles A., 98
Berrey, Ellen, 170
A Better Chance program, 191
Beyond the Melting Pot (Glazer
    and Moynihan), 169
biculturalism, 59–60
birth rates, demographic trends,
    3–5

black Americans, *see* African
    Americans
*Blackhorse et al. v. Pro-Football,
    Inc,* 105
The Black Star Project (Chicago),
    181
Blauner, Bob, 169–70
"Bleeding Heart" (Stoddard), 187
Bobo, Lawrence, 71
Bonilla-Silva, Eduardo, 6–8,
    66–67, 69, 71
Bourdieu, Pierre, 29
Brehm, Hollie Nyseth, 115–32
Brockovich, Erin, 129
Brown, Phil, 126
Bryant, Bunyan, 118
Buchanan, Pat, 16
Buck v. Bell, 89–90
Bullard, Robert, 117–18
Burgos, Adrian, 98
Burke, Meghan A., 7, 165–75
Burns, Ursula, 196–97

Cain, Herman, 168–69
California Civil Rights Initiative,
    16
Čapek, Stella, 125–26
Center for Constitutional
    Rights, 69
Centers for Disease Control and
    Prevention, 21–24
CEOs, diversity and, 191–205

Chapman, Duane "Dog," 68
Chenault, Kenneth, 196
Chicago
    The Black Star Project, 181
    Toxic Doughnut area, 118–20,
        129
Chicago White Sox sports
    team, 98
The Chosen (Karabel), 42
civil disobedience, 119
class
    college admission bias and, 42
    color lines and, 9–12
    diversity and new CEOs,
        193–97
    environmental inequality and,
        115–32
    self-fulfilling prophecy and,
        29
    success frame and, 28
    symbolic capital and, 30
    white trash, 83–94
Clean Air Act, 131
Clean Power Coalition (CPC), 120
climate change, 127–28
climate injustice, 128
Clinton, Bill, 119
Clooney, George, 84
colonization, 102–3
color-blind egalitarianism, 136
color blindness
    Alexander on, 184–85
    Bonilla-Silva on, 7–8

race consciousness versus,
        165–75
    whites and, 72–73
color-blind racism, 71
Columbus, Christopher, 100
Coming Apart (Murray), 91
Communities United Against
        Police Brutality, 139
Conley, Dalton, 45
Cooper, James Fenimore, 99
Cornell, Stephen, 13
The Cosmopolitan Canopy
        (Anderson), 171
criminal justice system
    mass incarceration, 177–88
    treatment of whites and, 69
Croll, Paul R., 73
cultural contexts
    environmental inequalities,
        115–32
    intersectionality, 150–51
    Native American mascots,
        95–113
    Trayvon Martin's death,
        133–49
    white trash, 83–93

Defense Appropriations Act
        (2010), Section 8113,
        101–2, 112–13
Deloria, Vine, Jr., 104
demolition derby, xxv–xxviii

Desmond, Matthew, 189
discrimination
    college admissions process,
        42
    environmental inequality and,
        122–25
    Merton on, 66–67
    mixed-race individuals, 58
discussion guide, 207–9
diversity
    American attitudes, 165–75
    at demolition derby, xxv–xxviii
    happy talk about, xxvii, 170
    new CEOs and, 191–205
    without oppression, 171
Diversity in the Power Elite
        (Zweigenhaft and
        Domhoff), 191
Domhoff, G. William, 17, 191–205
Dominicans, 50–58
DREAM Act, 15, 160
Duster, Troy, 91
Duvall, Clarence, 98

economic-based environmental
        inequalities, 120–22
Emirbayer, Mustafa, 189
environmental inequality
    about, 115–16
    discrimination-based
        explanations of, 122–25
    economic causes of, 120–22

emergence of, 116–17
expanding environmental
    justice, 125–29
GAO study, 117
global response to, 129–31
initial documentation and
    response to, 117–20
recommended reading, 131–32
environmental justice
    about, 117
    expanding, 125–29
    global response to, 129–31
    initial documentation and
        response to environmental
        inequalities, 117–20
    recommended reading,
        131–32
Environmental Protection
    Agency, 130
Erin Brockovich (film), 115–16, 119
ESL (English as a second
    language), 32
Espenshade, Thomas, 41–42
Espiritu, Yen Le, 62, 155–63
ethnicity, *see* race and ethnicity
eugenics movement, 87–91
exceptionalism, Asian American,
    40–43

Fair Housing Act, 130
Fair-Weather Illiberals, 66
Fair-Weather Liberals, 66

Federal Emergency Management
    Agency, 128–29
Fennelly, Katherine, 155–63
Ferguson, Faith, 126
Ferraro, Geraldine, 68
Fiorina, Carly, 193–94
Fortune magazine, 192
Fryberg, Stephanie, 103
future of race in America
    blurring or hardening of racial
        categories, 4–8
    class and lines of color and
        culture, 9–12
    demographic trends, 3–4
    recommended reading, 18–19
    underlying factors, 12–14
    white reaction and response,
        14–18

Gallagher, Charles A., 133–49
Gallup poll, 145
Gans, Herbert, 9–10
GATE (Gifted and Talented
    Education), 31–32
gender
    affirmative action and, 16
    diversity and new CEOs, 192,
        194, 197–203
    environmental inequality and,
        118, 126–29
    homicide victimization
        rates, 25

stereotype threat and, 38
General Accounting Office
    (U.S.), 117
Gerteis, Joseph, 73
Glaeser, Edward, 69
Glazer, Nathan, 169
globalization of environmental
    inequality issues, 127–31
golf, CEOs and, 198–99
Gonzalez, John, 103
Gould, Kenneth, 121
Griffin, Robert, III, 96
group activities, 210–12
Guiliano, Jennifer, 95–111
Gulya, Lisa, 150–51

Halloween costumes, 150–51
happy talk, xxvii, 170
Harjo, Suzan Shown, 104–5
Hartmann, Douglas, xxv–xxviii,
    3–19, 73, 170
Hattam, Victoria, 60
hegemonic whiteness, 71–72
Heise, Kia, 3–19, 45–47, 177–88
Higgins, Robert, 123
Hilton, Paris, 84
Hispanics
    American racial context and,
        54–60
    demographic trends, 3
    diversity and new CEOs, 192,
        194, 200–203

Hispanics (*continued*)
Dominicans and Puerto
Ricans, 50–58
environmental inequality and,
116, 119–20, 123
homicide victimization rates,
24–25
immigration trends, 8, 161
integration and, 60–63
interracial marriages and, 13
poverty and, 12
racial categories and, 46, 49–54
recommended reading, 63–64
SAT scores and college
admissions, 42
self-labeling strategies, 14
socioeconomic status, 69
homicide victimization rates,
21–25
Honors track (school), 31, 33–34
hoodie movement, 143–45
Hughey, Matthew W., 65–80
Human Rights Campaign, 192

immigration and immigrants
Alba's vision of America, 4–6
assimilation and, 5–6, 11–12
Bonilla-Silva on, 8
changes in policy, 12
demographic trends, 3–4
environmental inequality and,
115–16, 118, 123–24

ethnic identity and, 61–62
panel discussion regarding,
155–63
racial categories and, 46, 49
social mobility and, 10–11
individualism, 166
inequality, *see* racial inequalities
intermarriage
Alba on, 5
demographic trends, 8, 13
racial categories and, 13, 49
In the Shadow of Race (Hattam),
60
involuntary sterilization, 87–91
Isoke, Zenzele, 133–49

Jackson, Jesse, 68
Jacobson, Lenore, 39–40
Jewish population
college admissions process
and, 42
diversity and new CEOs,
203
Jiménez, Tomás, 61
Jung, Andrea, 192, 195
justifiable homicide, 139

Karabel, Jerome, 42
Key to Uncle Tom's Cabin
(Stowe), 86
Kochhar, Rajesh, 69

Krauss, Celene, 126
Krivo, Lauren J., 21–25

laissez-faire racism, 71
Lanham Act, 104
LaRoque, Angela, 103
Latinos, *see* Hispanics
Laughlin, H. H., 90
Lee, Jennifer, 27–44
Levin, Jonny, 96
Lewis, Amanda E., 78
Lewis, Aylwin, 198
Lin, Jeremy, 27–29
Logan, Enid, 133–49
Lynch, J. P., 156

Madison, James, 99
majority-minority society
    demographic trends toward, 3
    entrenchment of current
        lines, 7
    estimated date of, 16
Malcolm X Grassroots Movement,
    139
Manning, Alex, 189–90
Marshall, George Preston, 107
Martin, Trayvon, 133–49
mascots, Native American
    contemporary consequences,
        102–4
    controversy over, 95–97

debates over, 106–10
Defense Appropriations Act,
    101–2, 112–13
oppressive past and, 100–102
racialization of, 97–100
recommended reading, 110–11
trademark petitions, 104–6
Massey, Douglas S., 155–63
mass incarceration, 177–88
McCain, John, 194
McCoy, Sherilyn, 192
meritocracy, 170
Merton, Robert K., 29, 36,
    66–67
Meyers, John Tories, 98
Mills, Charles, 123
mixed-race classification, 13,
    51–59
model minorities, 9–10, 31
Morris, Aldon, 133–49
Moynihan, Daniel Patrick, 169
Muhammad, Khalil Gibran, 138
Murray, Charles, 91

NAACP, 183
Nagel, Joane, 13
National Congress of American
    Indians, 104
National Environmental Policy
    Act, 130
National Equality for All (NEA),
    74, 77

nationalism, 159–60

National Organization for
Working Mothers, 192

Native Americans
Defense Appropriations Act,
101–2, 112–13
environmental inequality
and, 116
identity changes and, 13
poverty and, 12, 101
racial categories and, 46
revisionist history and, 109
self-identifying as, 101
sports mascots and, 95–113
unemployment and, 101

Nee, Victor, 4–5

The New CEOs (Zweigenhaft and
Domhoff), 192

The New Jim Crow (Alexander),
xxiii, 172, 177–88

Niemonen, Jack, 65

non-zero-sum mobility, 5

Nooyi, Indra, 195

Nugent, Ted, 96

Obama, Barack, 15, 66, 68,
180–81

O'Brien, Eileen, 70

Occupy the Hood, 139

O'Leary, Hazel, 198

one-drop rule, 49, 54, 56

O'Reilly, Bill, 15

Pager, Devah, 69

Parsons, Richard, 196

Pellow, David N., 115–32

Phillips, Julie A., 21–25

Portes, Alejandro, 10–12

poverty
communities of color and, 12
homicide victimization rates
and, 25
Native Americans and, 12,
101

prejudiced discriminators,
66–67

prejudiced non-discriminators,
66

privilege, *see* white privilege

Pro Football, Inc., 104

*Pro-Football, Inc, Blackhorse
et al. v.,* 105

Puerto Ricans, 50–57

Pygmalion effect, 39–40

race and ethnicity
affirmative action and, 16
environmental inequality and,
115, 118, 128
future of race in America,
3–19
Hispanics, 49–64
as social construction, 45–47
social mobility and, 60–61
stereotype threat and, 38

race consciousness versus
color blindness, 165–75
race relations
downward assimilation and,
11–12
white racism and, 73
racial boundaries
blurring of, 4–6
determining, 46–47
hardening, 6–8
racial categories and, 55–56
racial categories
blurring of, 4–6
Gans on, 9–10
hardening of, 6–8
Hispanics, 60–63
intermarriage and, 13, 49
listed, 46
mixed-race individuals and,
13, 51–58
one-drop rule, 49, 54, 56
symbolic capital, 29–35
racial future of America, *see*
future of race in America
racial hierarchy, immigrants
changing, 5
racial identity
Asian Americans and, 62
assimilation and, 59–60
framing absolute rights and
wrongs, 65–80
Native Americans and, 13
whites, 70–79

racial inequalities
color blindness and, 7, 166–69
decline in, 71
eugenics movement and, 91
nature of, 166–67, 170
Racial Oppression in America
(Blauner), 170
racial profiling
challenging, 144
whites and, 69
racism
color-blind racism, 71
environmental inequality and,
122–25
established notions about,
65–80
homicide victimization rates
and, 25
institutional dynamics of, 170
laissez-faire racism, 71
recommended reading, 79–80
Radford, Alexandria, 41–42
Raines, Franklin, 197
Redskins sports team, *see*
mascots, Native American
*Remaking the American Main-
stream* (Alba and Nee), 5
residential integration, 5, 69
reverse racism, 17, 76
revisionist history, 109
Richards, Michael, 67–68
Rometty, Virginia, 192
rose-colored glasses, 156

Rosenthal, Robert, 39–40
Roth, Wendy, 14, 49–64
Rumbaut, Ruben, 11

SAT scores and college admissions, 42–43
Schnaiberg, Allan, 121
Schwalbe, Michael, 78
segmented assimilation, 10–11
self-fulfilling prophecy, 29, 35–37
Sen, Laura, 195
Shih, Margaret, 38
Simon, R. J., 156
Smith, Ryan, 71
Snyder, Daniel, 95, 106–7
social construction, race as, 45–47
social justice organizations, 139
social mobility
    communities of color and, 12
    downward, 9, 11–12
    non-zero-sum mobility, 5
    race and ethnicity and, 60–61
    upward, 9–11
socioeconomic status
    homicide victimization rates and, 25
    racial categories and, 55
Sockalexis, Louis, 98
sports, CEOs and, 198–200
Springwood, Charles Fruehling, 108–9

stand your ground laws, 133, 138, 146
Staurowsky, Ellen, 108
Steele, Claude, 29, 37–38
stereotype promise, 29, 37–41
stereotypes
    Asian American, 29, 37–41
    Halloween costumes and, 150–51
    immigrants changing, 5
stereotype threat, 29, 38
sterilization, involuntary, 87–91
Stoddard, Tom, 187–88
Stowe, Harriet Beecher, 86
Students Against Mass Incarceration, 184
success frame, 28–29, 34–35
Suh, Stephen, 133–49, 155–63
Suicide of a Superpower (Buchanan), 16
symbolic capital
    about, 29–31
    consequences of, 31–35

Take Our Country Back movement, 15
Tatum, Beverly, 142
Taylor, Dorceta, 118
Tea Party, 165–66, 168–69
Thompson, Don, 192
Thorpe, Jim, 98

Tough Choices (Fiorina), 193

Toxic Doughnut area (Chicago), 118–20, 129

Trademark and Trial Board, 104–5

trademarks, Native American mascots and, 104–6

Turner Strong, Paula, 108

unemployment, Native Americans and, 101

unprejudiced discriminators, 66

unprejudiced non-discriminators, 66–67

Vigdor, Jacob, 69

Wade, Lisa, 150

Ward, Lloyd, 198

Washington Redskins sports team, *see* mascots, Native American

Waters, John, 84

Waters, Mary, 13

What Would You Do? (TV series), 189

White Bound (Hughey), 70, 73

white debt, 74

white privilege

Bonilla-Silva on, 6, 8

Burke on, 171–72

fears of losing, 15

mixed-race individuals and, 59

Native American mascots and, 108

white racial identity, 70–79

whites (whiteness)

Burke on, 172

color-blind egalitarianism, 136

demographic trends and, 17

ethnicity and social mobility, 61

good whites/bad whites, 66–67, 70

hegemonic whiteness, 71–72

homicide victimization rates, 21–24

interracial marriages and, 13

poverty and, 12

racial categories and, 46

response to demographic changes, 14–18

reverse racism and, 17, 76

SAT scores and college admissions, 42–43

socioeconomic status, 69

sports mascots and, 98–99

Whites for Radical Justice (WRJ), 75, 77

white trash

eugenics movement and, 87–91

white trash (*continued*)
  origins of term, 85–87
  recommended reading,
    92–93
  term usage, 83–84
Whitman, Meg, 199
*Why Are All the Black Kids Sitting
    Together in the Cafeteria?*
    (Tatum), 142
Wing Young Huie, xxv–xxviii
Wise, Tim, 66
Working Mother magazine,
    193

Wray, Matt, 83–93
Wright, Beverly, 118

Yancey, George, 138

Zeskind, Leonard, 70
Zimmerman, George, 133, 138–41,
    143, 146
Zirin, Dave, 107
Zweigenhaft, Richard L., 17,
    191–205